Cultural Studies

A student's guide to culture, politics and society

Studymates

25 Key Topics in Business Studies
25 Key Topics in Human Resources
25 Key Topics in Marketing
Accident & Emergency Nursing
Constitutional & Administrative Law
Cultural Studies
English Legal System
European Reformation
GCSE Chemistry
GCSE English
GCSE History: Schools History Project
GCSE Maths
GCSE Sciences
Genetics
Geology for Civil Engineers
Hitler & Nazi Germany
Land Law
Law of Evidence
Maths for Engineers
Memory
Organic Chemistry
Practical Drama & Theatre Arts
Revolutionary Conflicts
Science for Engineers
Sex, Memory & Psychology
Social Anthropology
Social Statistics
Speaking Better English
Speaking Better French
Studying Chaucer
Studying History
Studying Literature
Studying Poetry
Studying Psychology
Tourism Studies
Understanding Maths
Using Information Technology

Many other titles in preparation

Cultural Studies

A student's guide to culture, politics and society

Philip Bounds

Lecturer in Cultural, Media & Film Studies

Studymates

First published in 1999 by Studymates, a Division of International Briefings Ltd,
Plymbridge House, Estover Road, Plymouth PL6 7PY, United Kingdom.

Telephone: (01752) 202301. Fax: (01752) 202331

Web site:	http://www.studymates.co.uk
Customer services email:	cservs@plymbridge.com
Editorial email:	editor@studymates.co.uk

Produced for Studymates by Deer Park Productions.

Typeset by PDQ Typesetting, Newcastle-under-Lyme

Printed and bound by The Cromwell Press Ltd, Trowbridge, Wiltshire.

Contents

List of illustrations

Preface

The aim of this book is to provide an introduction to Cultural Studies for students who are approaching the subject for the first time. There are a number of points to keep in mind before reading it:

- We will be chiefly concerned with the British tradition of Cultural Studies, though it will also be necessary to examine the ideas of non-British writers who have achieved a major influence in this country.
- Since Cultural Studies only began to take shape in the 1950s, you will probably be expected to acquire at least an outline understanding of the subject's history.
- We will therefore take a broadly historical approach to Cultural Studies, identifying the main theoretical trends which have shaped its development and specifying the periods in which they were most influential.
- It will obviously not be possible to consider everyone who has made an important contribution to the field, so we will illustrate the main theoretical positions by referring to the work of some key representative writers.
- It is important to read Chapter 1 before embarking on the rest of the book. It contains important introductory information on the aims, methods and history of Cultural Studies.
- This book should be of help to a very large number of students, since Cultural Studies is now taught across a broad range of subjects in the Humanities and Social Sciences. You may find it useful if you are enrolled on any of the following courses:

Secondary education
'A' level Communication Studies
'A' level Film Studies
'A' level Media Studies

Higher education
Art and Design
Cultural Studies
Communication Studies
Literary Studies
Media Studies
Sociology

I would like to thank the following people for their generous help: Hugh Alexander, Janet Alexander, David Bailey, Margaret Bounds, Peter Bounds, Dominique Fargeot (as ever), Ian Morgan and Edward Parr (who helped me compile the list of relevant websites).

My biggest debt is to my parents, Neville and Megan Bounds, to whom this book is dedicated.

Philip Bounds

Relevant Courses

This book is relevant to students enrolled on the following undergraduate degree schemes:

Communication Studies

Bournemouth University; Edge Hill University College; Goldsmiths College, University of London; University of Leeds; University of Leicester; University of Liverpool; University College, London; University of London Institute of Education; Napier University, Edinburgh; Queen Margaret College, Edinburgh; Sheffield Hallam University; University of Sunderland; Trinity and All Saints' College, University of Leeds; University of Wales, Cardiff.

Cultural Studies

Birkbeck College, University of London; University of Birmingham; Brunel University; University of East London; University of Lancaster; Liverpool John Moores University; London College of Printing and Distributive Trades; University of London Institute of Education; Manchester Institute for Popular Culture, Manchester Metropolitan University; Napier University, Edinburgh; Sheffield Hallam University; Staffordshire University; University College, Suffolk; Trinity and All Saints' College, University of Leeds; University of Warwick; University of the West of England; University of Wolverhampton.

Film Studies

Bolton Institute of Higher Education; Canterbury Christ Church College; University of Derby; University of Exeter; University of Glasgow; University of Kent at Canterbury; Liverpool John Moores University; London College of Printing and Distributive Trades; Napier University, Edinburgh; Sheffield Hallam University; Staffordshire University; University of Stirling; University of Wales, Aberystwyth; University of Warwick; University of Westminster.

Media Studies

University of Birmingham; Bournemouth University; University of Bradford; University of Brighton; De Montfort University; University of Derby; Falmouth College of Arts; University of Glamorgan; Glasgow Caledonian University; Goldsmiths College, University of London; University of Greenwich; Liverpool John Moores University; London College of Music and Media; London College of Printing and Distributive Trades; University of London Institute of Education; University of Luton; Salford University; Sheffield Hallam University; Staffordshire University; University of Stirling; University of Sussex; University College, Suffolk; Swansea Institute of Higher Education; Trinity and All Saints' College, University of Leeds; University of Ulster; University of Wales College Newport; University of Westminster; University of the West of England.

1

Understanding Culture

One minute summary – Cultural Studies seeks to analyse culture in all its forms, though it is especially noted for its work on popular culture. It has always been a highly political subject, in the sense that it explores the relationship between cultural activity and broader forms of social organisation. Most of the leading figures in the field would situate themselves on the radical left. In its first phase, between 1956 and 1969, Cultural Studies was shaped by the ideas of the 'New Left'. For much of the 1970s it was heavily influenced by Marxism. Since the early 1980s, it has been increasingly associated with the politics of the 'new social movements'. This chapter will help you understand:

- the definition of culture
- the politics of Cultural Studies
- the history of Cultural Studies

Defining Cultural Studies

Some writers have claimed that it is virtually impossible to provide a definition of Cultural Studies. They say the subject is simply too complex – or too shapeless and incoherent – to be summed up in a few brief sentences. There is doubtless an element of truth in this observation, but it obviously leaves the newcomer to the field in a difficult position. Without some sort of definition to guide us, we risk making no progress at all.

So while accepting that Cultural Studies is an unusually difficult subject to define, we can begin by saying the following:

► *Key definition* – Cultural Studies is the interdisciplinary analysis of all forms of cultural activity, with an emphasis on popular culture. It is a 'political' subject. This means that its central focus is on the relationship between cultural activity and broader forms of social organisation.

Our task in the rest of this chapter is to expand on this definition by answering three important questions:

1. How can we define culture?
2. What does it mean to describe Cultural Studies as a political subject?
3. How can we begin to think about the history of Cultural Studies?

Understanding culture

The definition of culture is just as controversial as the definition of Cultural Studies: no two writers seem able to agree about it. One of the best ways of avoiding this problem is to examine the ideas about culture that were prevalent when Cultural Studies was beginning to emerge in the 1950s, since these have continued to exercise a powerful influence over the field. Our best starting point is the early work of Raymond Williams. He famously argued in his book *The Long Revolution* that culture encompasses three related elements:

(a) a 'lived' element
(b) a 'documentary' element
(c) an 'ideal' element.

Investigating ways of life

The 'lived' dimension of culture is what Williams calls a 'particular way of life', or what we could simply define as the various modes of behaviour which prevail among social groups. Analysis of this level of culture could either focus on whole societies (Britain, for instance), or else on particular subsections of the wider community. Among the groups which have been of most interest to Cultural Studies are the working class, women, youth subcultures and media audiences.

Investigating communication

When we talk about the 'documentary' aspects of culture, we mean the various modes of communication which allow societies to convey and receive meanings. Cultural Studies has always operated with a very broad conception of human communication. Apart from analysing the complex of forms and practices which are self-evidently bound up with the transmission of meaning (language, the media, art etc), it also proposes that most phenomena in the social world can ultimately be regarded as systems of communication. It has, for instance, had much to say about the meanings inherent in fashion, the urban environment and the topography of institutions.

Investigating high culture

The 'ideal' dimension of culture encompasses what most of us would call 'high' or 'elite' culture. It means the body of analytic and creative work that has achieved a position of special prestige in our society, ostensibly because of its superior insights into the nature of the human condition. We will see that Cultural Studies has generally taken a sceptical attitude towards received ideas about high culture, though this does not mean that everyone in the field would wish to reject the category altogether.

Specifying the approach

Presumably we couldn't claim to be 'doing' Cultural Studies if we simply said the first thing about culture which came into our heads. What sort of approaches should we be prepared to take?

Our main objective is to identify what Raymond Williams has called the 'meanings and values' which culture serves to express. As we shall see in the next section, this sort of analysis is nearly always undertaken with a number of political questions in mind.

How about an example?

Imagine that you have been asked to write an essay about the cultural significance of going to the pub. You wouldn't be fulfilling your brief if you simply complained about the price of beer, described the pub decor or listed the records on the jukebox. But if you said that going to the pub involves a search for community in an increasingly fragmented society, you'd be well on the way to getting a good grade. Why? Because your attention would have shifted from the surface of human behaviour to precisely those 'meanings and values' which underpin it.

Which aspects of culture does Cultural Studies focus on?
Cultural Studies can explore any aspect of culture at all, from science to Shakespeare. In practice, however, it has usually been associated with analysing **popular culture**, which is one of the reasons why it is still so controversial.

Cultural Studies is a highly 'interdisciplinary' subject, in the sense that it has taken a variety of methods from other disciplines in the Humanities and Social Sciences and then used them for its own purposes. Some of these disciplines and methods are listed below.

Humanities	**Social Sciences**
Literary criticism	Political economy
Semiotics (the study of signs)	Ethnography
History	Psychology
Aesthetics	
Linguistics	

Fig. 1. The interdisciplinary basis of Cultural Studies.

The politics of Cultural Studies

So far, we have seen that cultural analysis involves the investigation of the 'meanings and values' which underscore culture in its lived, documentary, and ideal forms. But how is this done? The crucial point is that Cultural Studies approaches the analysis of meanings and values from a distinctively political perspective. Whenever we try to analyse a particular cultural activity, there are two questions that are likely to be uppermost in our minds:

- How can this cultural activity be seen as *reinforcing* support for the existing form of social organisation?
- Is there any way in which this cultural activity can be seen as *undermining* support for the existing form of social organisation?

Sometimes, these will be supplemented by a third question:

- What forms of cultural activity should we undertake to ensure that political change is achieved?

Advancing a radical agenda

Since it is now clear that ours is a highly political subject, we need to say something about the political ideas which have shaped its development. One of the most controversial aspects of Cultural Studies is its tendency to argue that political radicalism is an indispensable part of its academic identity. As a result, most of its leading figures have been aligned with the radical left, as we shall see in a moment.

There is no point denying that the political dimension of Cultural Studies is extremely contentious, though we need to remind ourselves that there are plenty of other subjects (such as Business Studies on the right and Women's Studies on the left) which also incorporate their political values into their core description. Whether or not this is desirable is not something we can debate here. The more urgent task is to show how the politics of Cultural Studies can help us to understand the *history* of the subject.

The periods of Cultural Studies

The best way of approaching the history of Cultural Studies is to try and identify the political ideas which have preoccupied its leading figures during the various phases of the subject's development. On this basis, putting it simply, Cultural Studies has moved through three distinctive phases:

1. In the period between 1956 and 1969 it was closely associated with the political movement known as the 'New Left'.

2. During the 1970s it was heavily influenced by Marxist ideas.

3. Since the early 1980s it has moved steadily away from Marxism and turned instead towards the politics of what are sometimes called the 'new social movements' (especially the feminist, anti-racist, and gay liberation movements).

Redefining socialism: Cultural Studies and the New Left, 1956-1969

Cultural Studies began to emerge in the period between 1956 and 1969, largely because of the efforts of three 'founding fathers': Raymond Williams (1921–1988), Richard Hoggart (b. 1918) and EP Thompson (1924–1993). It effectively became an independent subject in 1964, when Hoggart established the Centre for Contemporary Cultural Studies (CCCS) at Birmingham University. The work which Williams, Hoggart and Thompson produced at this time was powerfully influenced by their membership of the New Left, whose ideas we must now investigate.

What was the New Left?

The New Left was a loose grouping of intellectuals, students and political activists which emerged in Britain in the mid-1950s. Its main aim was to develop a new form of socialist politics. Historians usually describe it as a 'reformist' movement, in the sense that it was less interested in abolishing capitalism than in humanising it through radical reform. The major catalyst for the emergence of the New Left was a series of events in 1956, notably the Soviet invasion of Hungary, which seemed to prove that the attempts to build socialism in the USSR and Eastern Europe had gone badly wrong.

How did the New Left influence Cultural Studies?
There were two themes at the heart of the New Left's project. Both helped to set the agenda for early work in Cultural Studies. The first was the belief that existing forms of socialism had become excessively authoritarian, because they had concentrated political power in the hands of an elite. In response to this, the New Left tried to revive the idea that socialism could only work effectively if ordinary people ran it for themselves.

What was the other theme?
The New Left also wanted to restore a *cultural* dimension to radical politics. It felt that socialists had become narrowly preoccupied with issues of economic and political reform. It argued that one of the main tasks facing the post-war left was to create a new cultural settlement in Britain in which working-class ways of life would be more highly valued.

Summarising the period

In preparation for Chapter 2, we can summarise the most important developments in Cultural Studies between 1956 and 1969 thus:

(a) In books such as *Culture and Society* (1958), *The Long Revolution* (1961) and *Communications* (1962), Raymond Williams argued for the creation of a 'common culture' in Britain, rooted in the distinctive values of working-class life.

(b) In his book *The Uses of Literacy* (1957), Richard Hoggart assessed the likely impact of the newer forms of mass communication on 'traditional' working-class culture.

(c) In his book *The Making of the English Working Class* (1963), which examined the period between 1780 and 1830, EP Thompson tried to show how ordinary people had consciously created their own culture in response to the pressures of industrialisation.

Opposing capitalism: Marxism and Cultural Studies in the 1970s

Towards the end of the 1960s, Cultural Studies entered a new phase that was to last until the early 1980s. Its central feature was a renewal of interest in Marxist ideas, which had only been of minor influence on the New Left. Marxism is a political doctrine that has its origins in the work of Karl Marx (1818–1883) and Frederick Engels (1820–1895), the leading socialist thinkers of the nineteenth century. It favours the complete abolition of capitalism and the establishment of a socialist society, characterised by the 'common ownership of the means of production, distribution and exchange'. It assumes that this new society will be created by the working class, whose desire for political change will allegedly be stimulated by the 'class struggle' which already exists between ordinary people and their employers.

What was the effect of Marxism on Cultural Studies?
It ensured that opposition to capitalism became the subject's defining political characteristic (remember that the New Left had only been a 'reformist' movement). But also, more importantly, it provided cultural theorists with a distinctive method for analysing the role of culture in modern societies.

Meaning what, exactly?
The point we have to grasp is that there is much more to Marxism than its proposals for the abolition of capitalism. At its core is a theory of social change, usually known as **historical materialism**. This tries to explain how societies function and how they have developed over the course of history. Marxists would argue that the political and theoretical aspects of their project are closely related, in the sense that their opposition to capitalism is ultimately derived from the ideas about social change which historical materialism has proposed. As far as Cultural Studies is concerned, it is essential to note that historical materialism is also the starting point for the Marxist account of culture.

Understanding history

It would take an entire book in which to discuss the theory of historical materialism, but its central principles can be summarised as follows:

1. The most important feature of any society is the way that it organises its economic affairs.

2. The economic organisation of society is ultimately determined by the level of the 'productive forces': the resources used to produce wealth will always exercise the decisive influence on the structure of the economic system. The chief productive forces are raw materials, machinery, scientific knowledge and the ability of human beings to work (what Marxists sometimes call 'labour power').

3. There have been many different forms of economic organisation in the course of history, each corresponding to a different stage in the development of the productive forces. Marxists usually argue that society has passed through the following stages: primitive communism, slavery, feudalism, and capitalism.

4. There is nothing automatic about the transition from one form of society to another. Those who have benefited from the existing system will usually fight to maintain the *status quo*, especially if they belong to the 'ruling class' (that is, the group in society which owns and controls the means of production). It is only the oppressed classes which feel that they have an interest in establishing a new society.

5. Economic affairs always exercise the dominant influence over all other aspects of the social structure, though only 'in the final instance'. If we examine the political, legal, ideological and cultural levels of society (what Marxists sometimes call **the superstructure**), it is clear that their primary function is to reinforce support for the economic system.

Understanding culture

As the last point makes clear, the instinct of the Marxist is always to relate cultural processes to economic developments in the wider society. The Marxist will try to show how culture is used to legitimise the existing system, or occasionally how it can be used to subvert and undermine it.

In order to sharpen your understanding of how Marxism might try to link the spheres of economics and culture, think of the following examples:

(a) the way that the emphasis on 'individualism' in modern societies can be linked to the existence of the free market, which encourages competition between separate companies

(b) the way that the 'hedonistic' attitudes of post-war society can be linked to the existence of consumerism, which revolves around the sale of 'goods of pleasure' on the mass market

(c) the way that the emphasis on community in a lot of popular entertainment (soap operas, for example) tends to brush against the grain of capitalist society, by defying its support for individualist values.

Four schools of Marxist theory

Although Marxism was the dominant force in Cultural Studies during the 1970s, it did not succeed in unifying the field. What actually happened was that Cultural Studies subdivided into four competing schools of Marxist analysis, which can be roughly characterised as follows:

(1) *Culturalism*

This was probably the most optimistic school of Marxist theory, because of its sense of political complexity. Instead of simply dismissing popular culture as a site of political domination, it also emphasised the ability of ordinary people to adopt a dissenting or 'oppositional' perspective on capitalist society. Most of the leading culturalists were associated with the CCCS, which moved towards Marxism after Stuart Hall became its Director in 1969. The Centre was especially noted in this period for two reasons: (1) its use of the 'encoding/decoding model' to analyse the media, and (2) its work on youth subcultures.

(2) *Screen theory*

The objective of *Screen* theory was to develop a 'structuralist' form of Marxist analysis, which it then used to do two things: (1) explain why mainstream films and television programmes are able to reinforce support for capitalist society; and (2) explore the aesthetics of what it sometimes called 'counter cinema' (that is, the work of directors like Jean-Luc Godard who were central to the European avant garde). Named after the most influential film journal of its day, *Screen* theory is perhaps the most pessimistic movement in the whole of Cultural Studies.

(3) *Political economy*

The main purpose of work in this area is to examine the economic structure of the culture industry – ownership of companies and forms of investment for example. The idea is to assess the impact of commercial factors on the attitudes towards society which the industry promulgates. In the work they produced during the 1970s, writers like Peter Golding, Graham Murdock and Nicholas Garnham often concluded that the industry is forced by economic considerations into taking a conservative perspective on social affairs.

(4) *History*

Not all the leading writers in Cultural Studies have focused on contemporary issues. Some have written instead about the culture of the past. It would probably be going too far to say that there was a cohesive school of Marxist historiography during the 1970s, but there was certainly a network of historians who made an academic study of such topics as the history of the press, the nature of popular entertainment in the Victorian period, and the history of English.

Supporting the new social movements: Cultural Studies since the early 1980s

It was only during the early 1980s that Cultural Studies began to throw off the influence of Marxism. As we shall see in Chapter 6, there were two developments in particular which convinced many of the subject's leading figures that the socialist movement had finally run its course:

- the rise of Thatcherism and the New Right
- the belief that Western societies were entering 'new times' characterised by 'post-Fordism' in economics and 'postmodernism' in culture.

Understanding race, gender and sexuality

The shift away from Marxism has had two major consequences for Cultural Studies. They can be summarised as follows:

(1) *Support for the new social movements*

Many of the leading figures in the field have replaced their commitment to socialism with support for the new social movements, especially the feminist, anti-racist and gay liberation movements. Although recent work in Cultural Studies still owes an intellectual debt to Marxism, there is no question that its main political emphasis is on the need to resist discrimination against women, ethnic minorities and gays and lesbians.

(2) *The rise of 'cultural populism'*

Certain writers (especially John Fiske and Paul Willis) have recently been accused of taking a 'populist' approach to cultural analysis. It is said they combine uncritical celebration of popular culture with an attitude of frank indifference towards the serious arts. This too has been described as the direct result of the abandonment of Marxism: the cultural populists often seem to be compensating for their political disappointments by conceiving of culture as the site of a vigorous popular radicalism.

What next?

Our task in the rest of this book is to expand our knowledge of the main theoretical trends which have shaped Cultural Studies since its emergence in the 1950s.

- Chapter 2 will look at the effect of the New Left on Cultural Studies, focusing on the work of Raymond Williams.
- Chapters 3, 4 and 5 will examine the relationship between Marxism and Cultural Studies in the 1970s.
- Chapter 6 will cover the debates about Thatcherism and 'new times' which occurred in the 1980s.
- Chapter 7 will examine the idea of cultural populism.
- Chapter 8 will assess the impact of the new social movements on Cultural Studies, specifically by looking at work undertaken from a feminist perspective.

Helping you learn

Progress question

'Cultural Studies is the analysis of power within the context of meaning.' (John Hartley). Discuss.

Seminar discussion

1. Some people have argued that it is inappropriate to study popular culture in schools and colleges. How would you respond?

2. Is it acceptable for Cultural Studies to project a specific political identity?

Practical assignment

When you next watch your favourite television programme, think of some of the ways in which it reflects the wider organisation of society. Organise your thoughts on a page of A4.

Study and revision tips

1. Try and read a little more about the political ideologies mentioned in this chapter. Make yourself a little more familiar with some of the key thinkers and their ideas.

2. Buy a notebook and use it to record each new technical term in Cultural Studies which you come across.

2

The New Left

One minute summary – The most important figures in the early history of Cultural Studies were Raymond Williams, Richard Hoggart and EP Thompson. They were all associated with the political movement known as the New Left (see Chapter 1). Their work was especially influenced by the following aspects of New Left politics: (1) the desire to create a more democratic model of socialism, and (2) the desire to win increased recognition for the culture of the working class. Our focus here will be on the early work of Raymond Williams, who has ultimately had a bigger impact than Hoggart or Thompson on the development of Cultural Studies. This chapter will help you understand:

- Williams' vision of a common culture
- his attack on cultural elitism
- his proposals for reform of the media
- his relationship to the so-called 'culture and society' tradition

Envisaging a common culture

Williams' work of the 1950s and 1960s will be our main concern in this chapter. Among the books he wrote in this period were:

Culture and Society 1780–1950 (1958)
The Long Revolution (1961)
Communications (1962)

It is often argued that the most important feature of these books was their attempt to develop a theory of culture (see Chapter 1, Understanding Culture). However, it would be misleading to examine this aspect of Williams' work in isolation from his equally important interest in the *reform* of British culture. As we shall see, his vision of reform is organised around five propositions:

1. It is necessary to create a **common culture** in Britain – a 'whole way of life' shared by everyone – to replace the class-divided culture that exists at present.

2. The most desirable form of common culture is one in which the values of working people – specifically the ethic of 'solidarity' – are allowed to increase in influence until they serve as the foundation for the whole of national life.

3. The influence of working-class culture will only increase once ordinary people play a more direct role in the running of society.

4. This sort of democratic reform itself depends on the skills of 'advanced communication' being extended to the majority.

5. It is therefore necessary to call for extensive reform of our educational and cultural institutions, including common ownership of the means of cultural production.

Defining working-class values

As we have just seen, Williams looks forward to an age in which the values that are currently associated with the working class will have become dominant throughout society. He justifies this vision of a 'common culture' by distinguishing the values of working people from those of their 'bourgeois' counterparts; and then by explaining why the former should now be allowed to take precedence over the latter. Much of this work can be found in the famous Conclusion to *Culture and Society*, which remains one of the key documents in the history of the New Left.

The basic argument is that working-class culture is distinguished by its emphasis on 'community'. The member of the working class feels that his personal identity is inescapably bound up with that of the group to which he belongs. Not only does he conceive of progress in collective rather than individual terms, but his whole life is shaped by the need to show solidarity with others. His is a culture in which 'we are' is always given precedence over 'I am'.

Williams accepts that this outlook has yet to produce a body of 'intellectual or imaginative work', but he argues that it has been crucially important in the formation of a number of significant institutions. If we want to identify its central contribution to modern culture, we must look at 'the trade unions, the co-operatives and the Labour Party'.

Defining elite values

Why does Williams believe that the idea of community is so central to working-class culture?

At a very simple level he sees it as one of the main ways in which working people have defended themselves against poverty and political oppression. At the same time, however, he also regards it as part of a conscious effort to build an alternative to the culture of 'bourgeois liberalism'.

What precisely does Williams find objectionable about bourgeois culture?

His main criticism of bourgeois culture is that it is predominantly individualist. The member of the elite classes tends to define his identity *against* that of other people, rather than seeing himself as part of a wider community. His life is governed by the principle of self-interest.

Surely there's more to bourgeois culture than that?

Williams accepts that sections of the middle class are guided more by the 'idea of service' than by the ethic of individualism. He points to the example of society's 'upper servants' (especially those in positions of leadership), who believe that social stability must always take priority over the pursuit of self-interest. And yet, though he respects this outlook, he still insists that the working-class emphasis on solidarity is preferable. This is because it is more egalitarian than the idea of service, which is rooted in the assumption that the majority of people need to be helped because they are incapable of helping themselves.

Defending ordinary people

The ideas we have just examined are clearly at odds with mainstream assumptions about British society, especially the widely-held belief that working-class culture is somehow less advanced than that of the elite groups. Williams's response is to identify the ideas that have been used most frequently to disparage working-class culture, in order to expose them to critical analysis. He concentrates on the following:

- the idea of the 'masses'
- the idea of mass communication

'There are in fact no masses'

Williams insists that one of the most insidious methods of reinforcing prejudice against ordinary people is to imply that they belong to the 'masses'. He sees this term, which first came into widespread use in the early nineteenth century, as a response to three historical developments:

1. The growth of large urban populations in the aftermath of the Industrial Revolution.

2. The emergence of large factories.

3. The emergence of trade unionism and related forms of working-class politics.

Williams points out that when we describe people as belonging to the masses, we imply that their primary characteristics are 'gullibility, fickleness, herd-prejudice, lowness of taste and habit'. Yet his comments on how this sort of thinking can be challenged are surprisingly muted. The farthest he goes is to urge us to recognise that the idea of the masses is usually contrary to our own experience, in the sense that none of us would ever regard ourselves or our loved ones as being members of a mob. It is only when he shifts to the topic of mass communications that he recovers his critical edge.

Investigating mass communication

The argument here is that the idea of the masses has recently been bolstered by a powerful attack on the newer forms of commercial entertainment. Now that British culture is apparently dominated by the television, the cinema and cheap newspapers, it is frequently implied that ordinary people must be just as degraded as the popular forms which they enjoy. Although Williams is no admirer of commercial culture, he still realises that this argument needs to be contested. He does so in three ways:

1. He accepts that there is much that is shoddy and exploitative in contemporary popular culture, but rejects the idea that the prevailing forms of communications technology are somehow to blame. His own belief is that the uses to which technology is put will depend on the social and cultural context in which it operates, not on any intrinsic properties which it may possess. This allows him to argue that the electronic media may yet serve as the basis for a democratic system of communications, so long as it is liberated from the commercial forces which currently distort its output (see below, **Reforming the institutions**).

2. Williams argues that it is clearly mistaken to regard commercial culture as a window on the working-class mind, since most of its products are created by middle-class professionals.

3. He argues, further, that it is fundamentally misconceived to try and gauge the health of working-class culture by examining its documentary forms (films, newspapers, television programmes and so on), because these have never been central to the lives of ordinary people. Whereas documentary culture has always been important to other social groups, the working class has tended to channel its creativity into more practical activities – everything, as Williams puts it, from 'gardening, metalwork, and carpentry to active politics'.

Extending democracy

Now that we have discussed Williams' idea of a common culture, let's turn to the question of how it might be established. The New Left's interest in extending democracy now becomes of central importance. The crucial point, in Williams' opinion, is that it is only through extending its political power that the working class will come to exercise the decisive influence over the whole of national life. The emergence of a common culture is dependent, in the final analysis, on ordinary people having more control over their own affairs.

But the extension of democracy itself depends on a broader process of education, whose aim is to make the skills of 'advanced communication' available to the majority. This process is likely to be extremely complex (one of Williams' favourite words) because it means reforming most of the educational and cultural institutions which influence our capacity for self-expression.

Williams has much to say about every aspect of this 'long revolution', but we will concentrate here on his two most important themes:

1. His belief that the 'great tradition' (by which he simply means high culture) should be stripped of its elite connotations and integrated into the nation's 'common inheritance'.

2. His belief that it is possible to transform the media into the centrepiece of a more democratic culture.

Examining the 'great tradition'

It may, at first sight, seem strange that Williams regards the popularisation of high culture as one of the central aspects of democratic reform, but there are at least two reasons why this should be so.

First, he believes that high culture embodies the ideal of 'advanced communication' in its most sophisticated form, and should therefore serve as a model for democratic discourse as a whole. Second, he believes that there are various aspects of the great tradition, from the plays of Bertolt Brecht to the novels of DH Lawrence, which give extremely powerful expression to the sort of

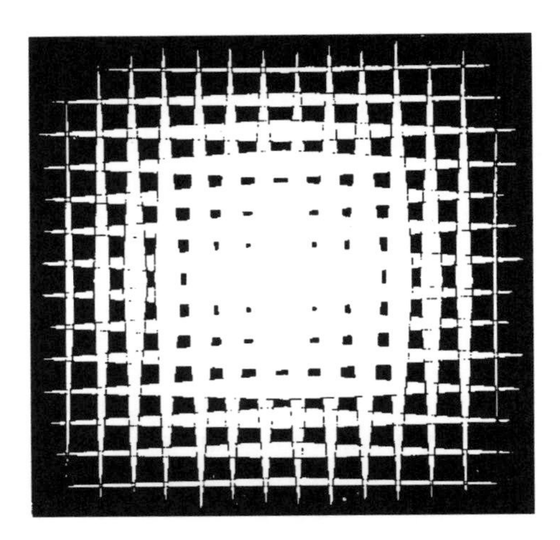

Fig. 2. The cover of the first edition of the *May Day Manifesto*, written by Raymond Williams, EP Thompson and Stuart Hall. Its publication in 1967 represented the high point of the New Left's intervention in British politics.

communitarian values that he hopes will underpin the common culture of the future.

Attacking cultural elitism

At the heart of Williams' writings on the great tradition is his critique of cultural elitism. His aim in a number of books, especially *The Long Revolution* and *Communications*, is to rebut the idea that high culture can only ever be the property of an educated elite. We shall focus here on his controversial analysis of dominant ideas about the nature of art. He points out, in a famous chapter in *The Long Revolution*, that it is common to describe the arts as a record of what he calls 'exceptional seeing'. It is assumed, in other words, that the artist makes a deliberate attempt to transcend his everyday perceptions in pursuit of aesthetic significance. Exceptional seeing is then contrasted with 'everyday seeing', which is held to be natural and spontaneous.

The problem with these ideas, in Williams' opinion, is that they create the impression of a yawning gap between art and everyday life. His attempt to close the gap is based on three assertions:

1. It is wrong, Williams says, to describe everyday perception as being somehow 'natural', because our ability to recognise things in the external world depends wholly on our having been taught how to do it.

2. It is wrong to argue that 'exceptional seeing' allows the artist to transcend everyday realities, because all art is indelibly shaped by the historical and political circumstances in which it is created.

3. Similarly, our perception of what constitutes great art is also shaped by political considerations, in the sense that each society will tend to privilege works which reflect its dominant values.

This argument, though clearly of a provisional nature, is still of the highest theoretical significance, because it represents the first occasion on which Cultural Studies took a sceptical approach towards the ideology of high culture. There is no space here in which to consider Williams' more specific arguments about the great tradition, but you might like to look at the following for yourself:

- his claim that the nineteenth-century novel reflected the 'crisis of the knowable community' at a time of rapid industrial expansion (see *The English Novel from Dickens to Lawrence*)
- his call for a new form of tragic drama that would explore the contemporary linkage between tragedy and revolution (see *Modern Tragedy*)
- his account, in *Drama from Ibsen to Brecht*, of the way in which certain forms of modern drama have tried to undermine the 'collective function' of the theatre.

Reforming the institutions

It will only be possible to establish a common culture once society has become more democratic, which in turn depends on the skills of 'advanced communication' being extended to ordinary people. This argument, as we have just seen, lies at the heart of Williams' conception of cultural change. But he also emphasises that the creation of a participatory democracy requires extensive reform of educational and cultural institutions, especially the media. It is to this issue that we must now turn.

Criticising the media

The media occupies a privileged position in Williams' early work. He believes that the press and broadcasting, with their unprecedented ability to disseminate information and broaden access to high culture, will ultimately play a pivotal role in shaping a more democratic society. Yet he is equally clear that the media is currently in the grip of commercial and governmental forces which serve only to encourage bias, trivia and escapism. When he surveys the existing state of the media, certain criticisms tend to reoccur:

(a) The notion of 'balance' which underpins public-service broadcasting is undemocratic. It presupposes that fair coverage should only be given to organisations and individuals that conceive of politics as a narrowly parliamentary activity.

(b) The press no longer supplies reliable information about important events, because reporters have begun to employ techniques whose main purpose is to elicit a partisan response. These include personalisation, the use of subtly prejudicial language, and the willingness to make dubious factual claims.

(c) Advertisements now occupy a disproportionate amount of space in commercial publications.

(d) Insofar as they imply that mundane commercial transactions can lead to fundamental improvements in the quality of life, advertisements are infecting British culture with the virus of escapism.

(e) The distinction between advertising and editorial matter is slowly being eroded, with the result that articles and reports now bear an increasing resemblance to advertisements.

Suggesting an alternative

But if the existing media system is so obviously undemocratic, what would Williams put in its place? Some writers have suggested that he favours complete public ownership of the media, but this is slightly misleading. It is certainly true that he wishes to protect the communications industry against the worst effects of market forces, but he also recognises that an entirely state-owned system would be open to two main abuses, which he identifies as follows:

- **authoritarianism**, where the state uses its influence over the media to limit freedom of speech
- **paternalism**, where a self-appointed elite is allowed to impose its judgements on everyone else.

Williams' objective is therefore to devise a sort of hybrid system, in which public ownership and media independence would exist alongside each other. He suggests that the following features should be central to any reformed system:

1. The means of cultural production (printing facilities, television studios etc) should be taken into public ownership, either at the local or national level. The responsibility for administering them should be devolved to a network of 'independent trusts', consisting of media professionals and members of the public.

2. The trusts should then lease the means of cultural production to what Williams calls 'independent professional companies', on a long-term basis.

3. There should be a number of different companies operating in each sector of the media industry, so as to avoid the undemocratic consequences of monopoly control.

4. The right to freedom of speech should be enshrined in law.

5. Insofar as bureaucracy poses as big a threat to freedom of speech as government interference, media companies should as far as possible be managed by their own workers.

Assessing the limits of free speech

Williams might claim that he wants the media to be as diverse as possible, but how far does his belief in freedom of speech really extend? What, for instance, is his attitude towards material which challenges the basis of accepted morality?
He seems fairly optimistic that once the media is liberated from commercial pressures, there will be a reduction in the demand for material of an especially lurid or sensational nature. At the same time, however, he recognises that there will always be cultural workers whose concerns are morally transgressive, and on the whole he feels that it is better to allow them their say than to censor them.

How does he justify this position?
In three ways. First, he points out that there is no hard evidence that transgressive material does any harm; second, by claiming that any act of censorship tends to undermine the principle of free speech;

third, by arguing that in a more democratic culture of the sort he envisages, cultural workers will feel accountable to their audience and will therefore be guided by a higher sense of public responsibility.

The 'culture and society' tradition

It is necessary, before we finish, to examine the way in which Williams tries to relate his work to a broader tradition of cultural criticism. In many of his early writings, especially *Culture and Society*, he argues that British intellectuals have been preoccupied with the idea of culture since the end of the eighteenth century, and that most of them have used it as a means of criticising the social order. This tradition of thought is too complex to be summarised here, so we must confine ourselves to three generalisations:

1. In the period between 1790 and 1870, when it was dominated by writers such as John Ruskin, Thomas Carlyle and William Morris, the tradition was bound together by its hostility towards industrialism.

2. The tradition experienced an 'interregnum' in the period between 1870 and 1914, when it came to accept the existence of industrialism but remained critical of its effects.

3. In the period between 1914 and the 1950s, when its key figures were writers such as FR Leavis, TS Eliot and George Orwell, the tradition was chiefly concerned with the cultural consequences of mass democracy.

The point we have to grasp is that Williams regards himself as an heir to this tradition, claiming to have reformulated some of its central ideas in the light of his socialist beliefs. The best way of understanding this claim is to glance at his assessment of the literary critic FR Leavis (1895–1978), who is often described as one of the key 'precursors' of Cultural Studies.

Summarising Leavis

Leavis was the most important figure in British literary studies for much of the period between the early 1930s and the late 1960s. At the heart of his work is a doctrine of cultural decline, which holds that European culture has undergone a rapid process of degeneration in the two centuries since the advent of industrialism.

Leavis is especially interested in the changing historical relationship between the writer and society. He argues that the structure of pre-industrial society was closely attuned to the needs of the writer, because it enabled him to cultivate the sort of 'poised' and 'restrained' sensibility which forms the basis of great literature. The problem, however, is that this state of affairs has completely disappeared under modern capitalism, which Leavis regards as the main enemy of the higher literary virtues.

One of the reasons why writers were more at home in pre-industrial society – the 'organic community', as Leavis likes to call it – was that it possessed a common culture. Works of literature were enjoyed by people from right across the social order, not just by an educated elite.

In his book *Culture and Environment* (1933), co-written with Denys Thompson, Leavis argues that the foundations of this common culture have been largely destroyed over the last two centuries, because:

1. The rise of industrialism has coarsened the outlook of ordinary people by depriving them of the opportunity to be creative in their work.

2. The expressive possibilities of the English language have been undermined by the rise of advertising, cheap fiction and the various other commercial forms which are typical of industrial society.

But what hope is there for literature in circumstances such as these? Leavis is clear that the organic community can never be recovered, but he refuses to surrender to outright pessimism. He believes that it is still possible for the writer to produce significant work, so long as he strives to identify with the spirit which animated European literature during the period before industrialism (this argument is largely taken from TS Eliot). And, finally, he also claims that the responsibility for safeguarding the literary inheritance lies with that small group of intellectuals (led by himself, of course) who have managed to resist the blandishments of industrial society.

Criticising Leavis

Of all the writers in the culture and society tradition, it was Leavis who exercised the biggest influence on Raymond Williams. And yet, by the time he came to write his early work, Williams had rejected most of Leavis's ideas about cultural history. In *Culture and Society*, for instance, he points out that:

(a) the idea of the organic community is largely a form of 'urban nostalgia'

(b) it is not true that all forms of industrial labour are devoid of creativity

(c) the wish to establish a literary elite has deeply undemocratic implications.

At the same time, however, it is clear that there are definite continuities between the two men's work. This is especially evident in Williams's efforts to reformulate the idea of a common culture from a radical perspective. Instead of consigning the common culture to a remote moment in an irrecoverable past, he regards it as a cultural goal that can only be achieved in a more egalitarian future. This explains why much of the early work in Cultural Studies is often described as a form of 'left Leavisism'.

Helping you learn

Progress questions

1. In what ways does the work of Raymond Williams reflect the wider objectives of the New Left?

2. '... the culture of the 'people' is iconised, and that of the nobs

tucked away out of sight' (Roger Scruton). Is this a fair assessment of Raymond Williams' early work?

3. What do you understand by the term 'left Leavisism'? Why can it be applied to the early history of Cultural Studies?

Seminar discussion

1. Would it be desirable to establish a common culture in Britain?

2. Is the idea of the 'masses' still a prevalent one?

Practical assignment

Think about the benefits and difficulties which might arise if the media were reformed as suggested by Williams. Write a brief essay summarising your conclusions.

Study and revision tips

1. Try and read Richard Hoggart's *The Uses of Literacy* to see how it compares with the work of Raymond Williams.

2. Find out some more about the so-called 'culture and society' tradition.

3

Media Analysis

One minute summary – Culturalist approaches to the media were characterised for much of the 1970s by a sense of political complexity. Instead of seeing the media simply as a conveyor belt for the dominant ideology, they emphasised that its messages are necessarily 'polysemic'. A less optimistic perspective was explored by writers in the field of political economy, most of whom argued that the media is forced by economic considerations into expressing broadly conservative views. This approach was often reinforced by cultural historians, who analysed the events which have led to elite domination of our media institutions. This chapter will help you understand:

- the encoding/decoding model
- Graham Murdock and Peter Golding's work on the economic structure of the media
- James Curran's account of the history of the British press

Introducing culturalism: the encoding/decoding model

As we have already seen, Cultural Studies was dominated in the 1970s by Marxist writers operating in the following areas: (1) culturalism, (2) political economy, (3) history, and (4) *Screen* theory. Our aim in this chapter is to introduce representative figures from the first three of these categories, specifically by looking at their work on the media. Before you read on, make sure you have understood the brief comments on Marxist cultural theory in Chapter 1.

The encoding/decoding model

Culturalism's main contribution to media theory in this period was the so-called 'encoding/decoding' model. Since these terms are not in everyday use, it is probably better to define them from the outset:

(a) 'encoding' refers to the process by which media texts are produced

(b) 'decoding' refers to the process by which media texts are interpreted.

The model, as we shall now call it, was developed at the CCCS by writers such as Stuart Hall and David Morley. However, it was rapidly taken up at a variety of academic locations. Perhaps the best way of approaching it is to see it as a cautious attack on the political pessimism which had characterised a lot of earlier work on the media, not least by the left. It is especially critical of two widely-held beliefs about the relationship between the media and ideology, which can be summarised as follows:

(a) Media texts are *solely* expressive of ideas and images whose purpose is to win support for the existing social system, that is, the so-called 'dominant ideology'.

(b) The media is invariably successful in transmitting this ideology to its target audience.

Against this conception of the ideological function of the media, the model asserts the following:

1. It is true that media texts are broadly expressive of the dominant ideology, but they should also be seen as **polysemic** (that is, they carry more than one meaning).

2. As a result, the media will not always be successful in 'contaminating' its audience with mainstream ideas. There will be times when the audience identifies with more progressive meanings.

3. These 'aberrant' readings are triggered by a contradiction between the moment of encoding and the moment of decoding.

Understanding polysemy

Let us examine the model in greater detail, beginning with the issue of polysemy, the idea that there is more than one meaning to be extracted from media texts. This is related to a broader point about the nature of ideology, derived from the work of the Italian thinker Antonio Gramsci (1891–1937). Gramsci argues that ideology can never consist exclusively of ideas which portray the *status quo* in a favourable light, because it has to win the support of thousands of disaffected people (women, blacks, the working class etc) who are inclined to hold beliefs of a broadly 'oppositional' character. Ideology can only be persuasive if it engages directly with these alternative beliefs, in order to 'frame' them in such a way that their political sting is neutralised. This is what Gramsci means by the term **hegemony**.

Examples

In order to clarify your understanding of this concept of ideology, consider the following examples:

(a) The argument which acknowledges that the free market can lead to exploitation, but also claims that the majority of exploitative employers are simply responding to the pressure of globalisation.

(b) The argument which acknowledges that gay men have made an important contribution to the history of the arts, but treats this as further evidence that they are incapable of leading normal lives.

(c) The argument which acknowledges that the western nations committed many unacceptable acts when they acquired their empires, but insists that the great virtue of imperialism was that it brought civilisation to undeveloped countries.

Making an active response

Why does this concept of ideology underpin the claim that media texts are often subjected to progressive decodings?

Because there is always a possibility that the audience will identify with the alternative meanings which the texts contain, even though this runs contrary to the media's intention.

Under what circumstances might this occur?
Usually when the audience begins to respond 'actively' to the media's messages. The model accepts that if people simply allow a tidal wave of sounds and images to wash over them, they will probably go along with the dominant meanings which the text tries to convey. It is only when they make a more dynamic response that they are able to subject the text to critical scrutiny, thus preparing the way for an alternative decoding.

And when does an active response of this sort become possible?
When the 'smooth' relationship between the text and its audience is disrupted, so that people begin to sit up and ask 'what's going on here?'

Disrupting the flow
Of the many circumstances which can prompt an audience into making an active response to media texts, the following are perhaps the most important:

- Firstly, when there is confusion about the meaning of a text. Stuart Hall points out that we rarely have trouble recognising the 'denotative' aspects of a media message (the things to which it refers), but we are occasionally uncertain about its 'connotative' dimension (the precise meanings it is trying to convey).
- Secondly, when the text's message blatantly contradicts the 'framework of knowledge' which the audience has derived from its social experience. As an example, think of the likely effect on a member of the unemployed of a party political broadcast that warns against the dangers of 'welfare dependency'.
- Thirdly, when a text is either produced by technology or makes use of techniques that seem inappropriate to the context in which it is decoded. (As an example, imagine the experience of watching one of the flashier Spielberg movies on a portable television in a deserted student common room.)

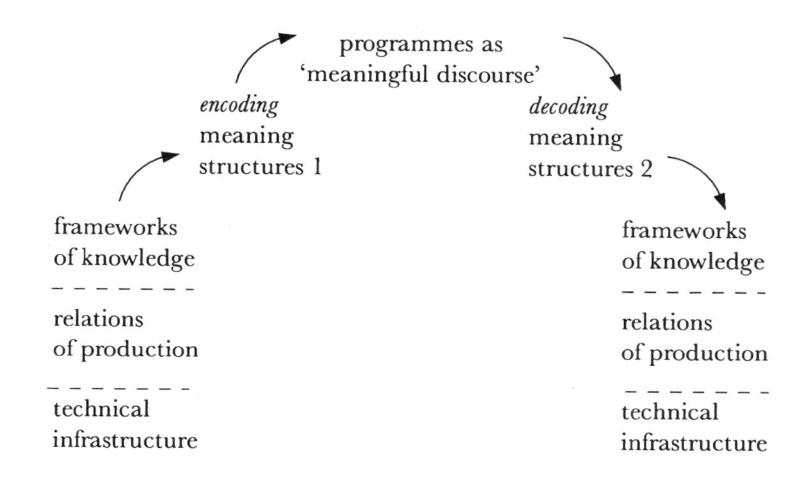

Fig. 3. Stuart Hall's attempt to sum up the encoding/decoding model in a diagram.

Classifying readings

On the basis of this argument, the model concludes that there are three ways in which a media text can be decoded or 'read', and these can be summarised as follows:

The preferred reading

This occurs when an audience simply goes along with a text's dominant message, making no attempt to interpret it from an alternative perspective.

The negotiated reading

This occurs when an audience broadly agrees with a text's dominant message, but also recognises that there are circumstances in which it would not apply.

The oppositional reading

This occurs when an audience completely rejects a text's dominant message, choosing instead to interpret it from an expressly dissident perspective.

Selling products: the political economy of the media

The main purpose of work on the 'political economy' of the media is to analyse how the media's economic structure affects its approach to politics. The best way of introducing this branch of Cultural Studies is to examine the collaborative work of Graham Murdock and Peter Golding, specifically their books and essays from the 1970s.

Concentrating ownership

At the core of Murdock and Golding's work are three related arguments, which can be summarised as follows:

1. The media is usually forced by economic considerations into expressing a conservative perspective on social affairs. (Note the absence here of any culturalist optimism about the polysemic character of media messages).

2. The media's political message is primarily affected by the high degree of 'concentration' which characterises its economic structure. Most sectors of the communications industry are now controlled by a small number of very large organisations.

3. Concentration is important not only because it places the media directly under the control of society's elite groups, but also because it produces an obsession with profitability which tends to have undemocratic consequences.

Understanding concentration

Murdock and Golding argue that the 'shift towards concentration' has been gathering pace in most sectors of the economy for over a century, but that it has been especially pronounced in the postwar period. They prove the point in relation to the communications industry by referring to the relevant 'concentration ratios', which measure the share of the market controlled by the top five companies in each sector. By the early 1970s, for instance, concentration ratios had risen to 71% in the newspaper industry, 78% in the cinema industry and 65% in the record industry.

This level of concentration has developed because of three related processes, which Murdock and Golding refer to as follows:

integration

diversification

internationalisation

Integrating companies

Integration occurs when different companies in the same sector of the economy combine into a single unit, either because of a takeover or a merger. It usually takes one of two forms. 'Horizontal' integration refers to the process by which companies of a *similar type* are joined together, as when Penguin Books was bought by Pearson Longmans in the early 1970s. 'Vertical' integration refers to the fusion of companies that had previously dealt with different aspects of the same production process. An example was the take over of the Associated British Picture Corporation (which exhibits films) by EMI (which makes them) in 1969. Murdock and Golding argue that integration is driven by the following factors:

1. The wish to offset competitive pressures.

2. The wish to maximise efficiency by increasing the size of productive units.

3. Where vertical integration is concerned, the wish to counteract damaging economic developments (especially price increases) which originate in different areas of the same sector.

Diversifying interests

Diversification occurs when there is a measure of convergence between companies operating in different sectors of the economy. It can either be direct (as when companies are formally combined) or indirect (as when separate companies undertake joint-investment initiatives or establish 'reciprocal shareholdings and interlocking directorships'). A slightly bizarre example from the media sector is

EMI's decision to buy the Golden Egg chain of restaurants in the 1970s. Murdock and Golding argue that diversification tends to occur at times of economic presssure, when companies feel that they can only maintain their existing rate of profit by expanding into new areas.

Internationalising operations

Internationalisation can be said to occur when a company begins to play a significant role in the economy of a foreign country, either by exporting goods or through direct investment. Media companies in Britain are generally held to have decisively extended their international reach in the 1970s, not least because of British entry into the EEC in 1972.

Reinforcing the mainstream

But why do economic processes of this sort tend to force the media into expressing 'establishment' opinions? At a simple level it is because they concentrate the ownership of media companies in the hands of the extremely wealthy, though this is not an argument which Murdock and Golding emphasise.

More important is the way that concentration leads to irresistible pressure to increase the size of the media audience, so that an adequate return on very high levels of investment can be guaranteed. Murdock and Golding hold that this is politically undesirable for the following reasons:

(a) Media companies assume that they can only be successful in the marketplace if they reflect the beliefs of their target audience. Since the majority of people are wedded to the values of capitalism (otherwise the system could not exist), this ensures that it is only bourgeois ideology which gets a hearing.

(b) There is a tendency on the part of the media to endlessly recycle successful products, simply because of their proven commercial record. This usually takes one of two forms. There is firstly what Murdock and Golding call 'multi-marketing', whereby 'successful products in one medium are converted into a form amenable to marketing in another medium'. Secondly, there are also persistent attempts to revive public interest in the media culture of the past, usually on the basis of an appeal to nostalgia.

(c) Commercial pressures have a trivialising effect on the coverage of political events, leading to frequent attempts to blur the distinction between entertainment and current affairs.

(d) When media companies seek to internationalise their audience, they often exacerbate a situation in which the culture of many Third World countries is dominated by the West. This is the problem of what some writers have called **cultural imperialism**.

Attacking the 'Whig' interpretation of press history

As our example of a Marxist approach to the history of the media, we will look at James Curran's influential work on the development of the British press. Curran's method is to attack the so-called 'Whig' interpretation of press history, which still tends to predominate among orthodox historians (Whig can be regarded in this context as a synonym for liberal). This has three main components.

- It assumes, in the first place, that freedom of the press is now an established feature of British society.
- Secondly, it argues that the press only won its freedom after a long campaign against repressive laws in the early nineteenth century, led by members of the liberal establishment.
- And, thirdly, it insists that when the press achieved its 'financial independence' in the period after 1860 (largely because of advertising), its ability to print what it liked was powerfully reinforced.

Formulating an alternative

Curran responds to the Whig interpretation of press history in the following ways:

Fig. 4. A selection of mastheads from the radical press of the early nineteenth century.

- He disputes the view that the campaign against censorship was led primarily by middle-class liberals. Instead, he argues that the radical press of the early nineteenth century played a much more important role in resisting repressive laws.
- He doesn't believe that the repeal of these laws resulted in the establishment of a free press. By the 1850s, when the relevant legal changes were taking place, new and more effective methods of regulating the press had begun to emerge.
- He argues that most of these methods were economic. As a result of the technological and financial changes which swept through the newspaper industry in the late nineteenth century, ownership of the press was concentrated in the hands of the elite classes. The radical press was one of the first casualties of the new system.

Introducing the radical press

Let us examine this argument in more detail. Curran's first point is that the campaign against censorship was spearheaded by the radical press, not by concerned members of the liberal middle-classes. But what precisely does he mean by the radical press? He is referring to such working-class newspapers as the *Political Register*, *Northern Star*, *Black Dwarf*, *Poor Man's Guardian* and *Republican*, which achieved a national circulation in the period between 1780 and 1850. Their main purpose was to reflect the upsurge in popular protest that occurred at this time.

Curran emphasises that it was relatively easy for the working-class movement to sustain a variety of newspapers, if only because:

(a) launch costs in the early nineteenth century were extremely low. Many radical newspapers were printed on hand presses, which could be bought for £10

(b) most of the people who contributed to the radical press were unpaid activists, happy to work for nothing

(c) radical newspapers were usually sold on the streets by unemployed volunteers, who also received no payment.

Resisting state power

The state had recourse to a number of laws in its attempt to suppress the radical newspapers. One of the most important was Fox's Libel Act of 1792. This was worded so vaguely that nearly any piece of robust journalism became vulnerable to a charge of either sedition or libel. Of even greater enormity was the series of laws that established the so-called 'taxes on knowledge', the first of which had appeared on the statute books as early as 1712. These stipulated that publishers had to pay a tax on paper, in addition to hefty duties on every newspaper they sold and every advertisement they accepted for publication. Their objective was to try and ensure that newspapers were too expensive for ordinary people to either own or read.

Curran suggests that the radical press resisted these laws in the following ways:

- It tended to provoke the state into bringing prosecutions for libel, because it knew that juries were reluctant to convict under the terms of Fox's Act. It also knew that circulation was likely to increase once a newspaper had been accused of sedition. The net effect of all this was to bring the existing law into disrepute (it was eventually modified in 1843).
- It refused to pay the taxes on knowledge, knowing that its extensive network of underground distributors would ensure that papers were read. This too tended to bring the law into disrepute.
- It set up a series of 'victim funds' which provided for the family of any activist who had been sent to prison.

The final stage in the struggle

The state made a number of changes to the law in 1836, each intended to strengthen its hand against the radical press. It reduced the taxes on knowledge by 75% (thereby increasing the likelihood of compliance), as well as taking new powers to raid the premises of recalcitrant publishers. But even this didn't work. It was perfectly true that the radical newspapers increased in price, but their supporters ensured their survival by clubbing together to buy individual copies. Knowing that its attempts to regulate the press had failed, the state repealed the taxes on knowledge in the 1850s.

Exerting control through economics

This was clearly a heroic campaign. So why doesn't Curran believe that the repeal of repressive laws led to the establishment of a free press?
The big irony, in Curran's opinion, is that the repeal of these laws brought about a transformation in the economics of the newspaper industry. This had the effect of concentrating the ownership of the press in the hands of the very wealthy.

What does Curran have in mind?
Demand for newspapers underwent a massive increase once the taxes on knowledge had been abolished. This led to the development of more sophisticated forms of print technology. Examples included the Hoe printing press in the 1860s, Hattersley's composing machine in the 1880s and the linotype machine in the 1890s. Most of this technology could only be afforded by companies which owned a significant amount of capital. Just as important were the massive amounts of advertising revenue that flowed into the industry in the period after 1860. Since most of it was directed towards the establishment press, the radical newspapers could now be priced out of the market.

How can Curran's argument be summed up?
At the very moment when the state was abandoning its efforts to regulate the press, a new and more effective 'control system' was in the process of being established. It remains in place today.

Helping you learn

Progress questions

1. How successful is the encoding/decoding model in challenging the idea that the media simply exists to transmit the 'dominant ideology'?

2. Why do Graham Murdock and Peter Golding argue that any account of the media's political function should be rooted in an analysis of its economic structure?

3. In what sense do James Curran's historical writings provide an alternative to the 'Whig' interpretation of press history?

Seminar discussion

1. Would you agree that the economic organisation of the media is inimical to political democracy?

2. What are the factors which make it difficult for the radical press to achieve a large circulation?

Practical assignment

Read a little more about Antonio Gramsci's theory of hegemony, then watch a cross section of news and current affairs programmes. Consider whether your understanding of these programmes has been sharpened by Gramsci's ideas.

Study and revision tips

1. Be sure you understand why culturalism and political economy are usually regarded as conflicting approaches to media analysis.

2. Choose a handful of vivid historical examples which you can use to illustrate Curran's work on the press.

4

Subcultures

One minute summary – The analysis of youth subcultures has been a central part of the 'culturalist' tradition. The classic theory of subcultures was developed by the Centre for Contemporary Cultural Studies (CCCS) in the 1970s. It holds that groups like the teddy boys, mods and skinheads allow working-class youths to express 'symbolic resistance' to aspects of their class experience. This view has been challenged by work on more recent subcultures, such as punk and rave. Punk has been described as an explicitly political movement, intent on destroying 'media society'. Rave culture has been analysed in the context of the rise of the New Right. This chapter will help you to understand:

- the CCCS's theory of subcultures
- the CCCS's understanding of teddy boys, mods, skinheads and punks
- the idea of punk as a 'political' subculture
- recent work on the rave scene

Symbolic resistance: the CCCS and youth subcultures

As we saw in the last chapter, one of the central aspects of culturalism is the belief that popular culture is often the site of 'resistance' or 'opposition' to capitalist society. This belief is most apparent in the analysis of subcultures undertaken by the CCCS. The essentials of the CCCS's theory can be found in the following works, though you should bear in mind that there are differences of emphasis in each:

Stuart Hall and Tony Jefferson (eds), *Resistance through Rituals:*

Youth Subcultures in Post-War Britain (1976)

Paul Willis, *Profane Culture* (1978)

Dick Hebdige, *Subculture: The Meaning of Style* (1979).

If we had a single sentence in which to summarise the insight that informs this body of work, we could say something like this:

► *Key concept* – Most subcultures involve an attempt by working-class youths to employ style, ritual and other forms of personal behaviour to express 'symbolic resistance' to aspects of their class experience.

In order to understand this definition more fully, we must now look at the following matters:

subcultures and class
style and symbolic resistance
subcultures and race

Facing the realities of class

One feature in particular distinguishes the CCCS's work on subcultures from that of other writers. This is the belief that subcultural activity originates in youthful dissatisfaction with various aspects of working-class experience. If we want to understand why groups like the teddy boys, mods and skinheads behaved as they did, we need to grasp that they were all working-class youths trying to deal with working-class problems. *Note*: although the CCCS is aware of middle-class subcultures such as the hippies, most of its work focuses on the predominantly working-class groups, such as the teddy boys, mods and skinheads.

According to the CCCS, the purpose of subcultures is to allow young people to express opposition to the class-related difficulties which they face. Let us be clear about what this means. It is not being suggested that subcultures are trying to change the existing system, least of all through political action. It is rather that they develop styles, rituals and other forms of behaviour which allow them to 'advertise' or 'display' their dissatisfaction to the rest of the world. This is what we mean by **symbolic resistance**.

Dressing up for status: the teddy boys

We can illustrate these ideas by looking briefly at the teddy boys of the 1950s. In an essay in *Resistance through Rituals*, Tony Jefferson argued that the emergence of the teds was caused by two class-related factors:

1. The fact that most of the teds belonged to the 'lower' working class and therefore existed on the margins of the economic system.

2. The breakdown of the 'extended kinship network' in the early post-war period. Jefferson refers here to the effects of the so-called 'slum clearance' of the 1940s and 1950s. Replacing back-to-back houses with impersonal high-rise flats tended to destroy the sense of community which had been central to 'traditional' working-class life.

In Jefferson's opinion, the teds responded to these difficulties in two ways:

Dress

To compensate for their lack of status, they developed an extravagant style of dress which incorporated the sort of clothes worn by upper-class youths in the Edwardian period. These included drape jackets, velvet collars, suede shoes and drainpipe trousers.

Territorialism

As a means of countering the breakdown of community life, they developed an extreme form of 'territorialism'. Most obviously, this involved the use of violence to 'defend their patch' against anyone they saw as alien.

Using style

As we have just seen in our comments on the teddy boys' choice of clothes, the CCCS believes that style is one of the most effective means for subcultures to express symbolic resistance to the wider society. Although its analysis of subcultural style is often very complex, there are two aspects of it worth singling out:

1. The idea that subcultural style involves a form of 'intentional' communication.

2. The use of bricolage in expressing symbolic resistance.

Intending to communicate

According to the CCCS, subcultural style is a form of 'intentional' communication. It is clear to everyone that an enormous amount of thought has gone into the image which a subculture tries to project. This is one of the key factors which distinguishes the member of a subculture from mainstream society. Although everyone's appearance conveys a meaning of one sort or another, the majority of people do not give the impression that their stylistic choices are the product of much conscious deliberation.

The CCCS feels that the intentional aspect of subcultural style is inherently progressive. By forcibly reminding us that our personal appearance is something we can control, subcultures prove that there is nothing natural or inevitable about the range of factors which influence human behaviour. This, in turn, goes a long way towards undermining the idea – often invoked in mainstream ideology – that human nature should be seen as static, natural and unchangeable.

Appropriating signs

When the CCCS comes to analyse the precise ways in which subcultures use style to express oppositional meanings, it places considerable emphasis on the idea of **bricolage**. This term is borrowed from the anthropologist Claude Levi-Strauss, who used it in his work on primitive societies. It refers to the way in which a sign already possessing a stable meaning can nevertheless have its meaning transformed, simply by being used in a novel context. The CCCS's argument is that bricolage is the basis of subcultural style.

As an example, let us think again of the teddy boys. It is clear that when they 'appropriated' the sort of clothes that had previously been worn by upper-class Edwardian youths, they were changing the meaning they conveyed from something like 'affluence' to something nearer 'opposition to low status'.

Why is the idea of bricolage important?
Because it shows that subcultures are not only 'oppositional' in what they say, but also in the way they say it. Quite apart from being critical of their class experience, they also show their irreverence towards mainstream society by appropriating its signs and bending them to new purposes. This is what Dick Hebdige has in mind when he says that subcultural activity involves a form of 'semiotic guerilla warfare' (the phrase was originally Umberto Eco's).

Forging solidarity
There is one other matter, closely related to the CCCS's analysis of style, which we should look at before we move on. This is the argument that white subcultures have always been heavily influenced by the culture of young blacks, especially those of Afro-Caribbean origin. It can be summarised as follows:

1. Many members of white subcultures feel a sense of affinity with young blacks, because of their shared history of oppression.

2. This sense of affinity often expresses itself in aesthetic form, with white subcultures appropriating aspects of black style and listening to black music.

3. Not all subcultures are entirely comfortable about their relationship with black culture. Although some, such as the mods and punks, show open solidarity in their attitude towards black youths, others go out of their way to deny having been influenced by them. The skinheads are the obvious example.

4. This means that certain subcultures have a sort of schizophrenic attitude towards black culture, owing it a stylistic debt but also holding openly racist attitudes.

5. The interchange between white subcultures and black youth is ultimately progressive, regardless of the racial attitudes of individual subcultures. This is because it points to the creative possibilities of a collapse of the boundaries between black and white culture.

This table contains the following information: (1) the aspects of working-class experience to which the mods, skinheads and punks were responding; (2) the forms of symbolic resistance which they employed; and (3) the ways in which they were influenced by black culture.

MODS	
Responding to: The impact of consumerism on working-class life	*Forms of symbolic resistance:* (1) Extreme vanity (often linked to the cultivation of male effeminacy) (2) 'Conspicuous consumption' (that is, the attempt to parody the logic of consumerism by resorting to excessive forms of personal expenditure) *Black influence:* Imitation of 'sharp' look associated with Jamaican 'rudies'
SKINHEADS	
Responding to: (1) Disappearance of unskilled jobs in the manufacturing sector (2) Disappearance of 'traditional' working-class communities	*Forms of symbolic resistance:* (1) Adoption of a highly masculine style which deliberately exaggerated the look of the 'traditional' factory worker (2) Territorialism *Black influence* Early on, some stylistic nods to the Jamaican rudies, such as the wearing of 'pork-pie' hats. (Note, however, that the skinheads soon dissociated themselves from black youths and became an openly racist subculture)
PUNK	
Responding to: Pervasive sense of imminent social collapse	*Forms of symbolic resistance:* The adoption of a highly fragmentary style intended to express 'chaos at every level' (Dick Hebdige). Think, for instance, of the juxtaposition of safety-pins, bin liners and spiked hair against traditional fabrics such as tartan *Black influence:* (1) Enthusiasm for reggae (2) Some stylistic nods towards rastafarianism

Fig. 5. Applying the theory: the CCCS on mods, skinheads and punks.

Subcultures and the CCCS: final questions

Why should the CCCS want to emphasise these points?
Remember that the CCCS consists of predominantly Marxist writers who believe that a new society will be created through 'class struggle'. By arguing that subcultures express symbolic resistance to aspects of working-class life, it can create the impression that working-class youths are involved in a sort of class struggle at the level of culture.

Are all the members of the CCCS in agreement about the interpretation of subcultures?
Not necessarily. Remember, individual writers often differ over points of interpretation. In particular, some members of the CCCS have attacked its theory of subcultures from a feminist perspective. The most important example of this is Angela McRobbie's article *Settling Accounts with Subcultures: A Feminist Critique* (see Chapter 8).

Understanding mods, skinheads and punks

If you want to understand how the CCCS applied its theory to the most important subcultures of the 1960s and 1970s (namely the mods, skinheads and punks), please look at the table on page 60.

Subverting the spectacle: the challenge of punk

In the remainder of this chapter, we will look at some of the more important ways in which the CCCS's ideas have been reworked. Much of this reworking has been prompted by the emergence of new subcultures. These include punk, new romanticism and rave, which could not easily be analysed in terms of the existing theory. In this section, we will see how subcultural studies have responded to punk. (Note, however, that the CCCS has also tried to analyse punk, as can be seen in the table).

Moving away from the CCCS

The attempt to understand punk has been undertaken by a number of individual writers, rather than by a 'school' of related theorists.

The most important are probably Iain Chambers (see *Urban Rhythms: Pop Music and Popular Culture*), Jon Savage (see *England's Dreaming: Sex Pistols and Punk Rock*) and George McKay (see his chapter on the band Crass in *Senseless Acts of Beauty: Cultures of Resistance since the Sixties*). Although they have not really developed a shared understanding of punk, there are at least two arguments which distinguish them from the CCCS:

1. The first relates to the issue of class. According to writers like Chambers, Savage and McKay, punk was never simply a movement of working-class youth. It was more the creation of a group of radical bohemians, whose aim was to introduce a note of revolutionary anger into British popular culture. Of special interest here is the role of former art students such as Malcolm McLaren, Vivienne Westwood and Jamie Reid in shaping the music and image of the Sex Pistols.

2. The second point follows on neatly from the first. If the objectives of people like McLaren, Westwood and Reid were explicitly revolutionary, then it makes little sense to analyse punk in terms of the CCCS's idea of symbolic resistance. Instead, it should be seen as a movement which deliberately set out to achieve political change.

Defining anti-aesthetics

This raises the question of the politics to which punk has been linked. According to the writers we have been looking at, punk took its basic ideology from the 'anti-aesthetic' tradition in European politics. This tradition embraces such art movements as Dadaism, Fluxus and the Situationist International. It can be defined by its commitment to a single idea: the belief that political progress – usually conceived in Marxist or anarchist terms – can only take place once the institution of art has been destroyed.

Opposing the spectacle

The most important anti-aesthetic movement to influence punk was probably the Situationist International (SI), which existed in Europe between 1957 and 1972. Among its key ideas were these:

- In the modern world, the best way of achieving political change is to work towards the transformation of 'everyday life', which the SI broadly defines as the sphere of leisure.
- The goal is to turn everyday life into a sort of permanent carnival. If this occurs, ordinary people will come to regard the tedium of their working lives as intolerable. This will sharpen their opposition to capitalism.
- Unfortunately, everyday life is now dominated by a vast network of images, conveyed to us by the media and other sources. This is what the SI calls the 'Spectacle'.
- Since the Spectacle robs ordinary people of their ability to live creatively, the only option is to destroy it. This is what the SI has in mind when it talks about destroying art.
- A variety of cultural strategies needs to be developed if the Spectacle is to be destroyed. One of the most important is that of **detournement**, the practice of taking elements from existing works and rearranging them into new configurations, in order to make them look absurd.

Doing it yourself: Situationism and punk

There is no question that people like McLaren, Westwood and Reid were heavily influenced by Situationist ideas. Nor is there any doubt that they saw punk as a means of infiltrating these ideas into the mainstream. But how was this done? In the opinion of the writers we have been looking at, punk was influenced by situationism in at least three ways:

Primitivism

The punks believed that music should be as raucous and unsophisticated as possible, so that no one would be excluded from playing it. 'Do-it-yourself' was the order of the day. This 'primitivist' bias has been seen by writers like Chambers, Savage and McKay as all part of the effort to destroy the credibility of media society.

Visual style
The technique of detournement was central to the sartorial and graphic styles which punk tried to develop. As an example, think of Jamie Reid's graphic for the Sex Pistols' single *God Save the Queen*, in which a safety pin has been inserted into the monarch's lip.

Public scandal
The punks wanted to shock people into an awareness of the tedium which pervades media society. One of their ways of doing so was to orchestrate public displays of scandalous behaviour. This was an old Situationist technique. Think of the Sex Pistols' appearance on the *Bill Grundy Show* in 1976, when they exposed a primetime audience to a cheerfully gratuitous display of boorishness, blasphemy and bad language.

Punk: some final questions

Are there any other ways of seeing punk as a political subculture?
Some people have written about punk from the perspective of feminist politics. Iain Chambers, for instance, points to how punk's sartorial style tended to 'de-sexualise' the body. Amongst other things, this allowed the punks to pose a challenge to existing gender identities. Not only were male punks often conspicuously unmasculine in their appearance, but female punks took the opportunity to transcend 'mainstream' forms of sexual display.

And what about Mrs Thatcher? Was punk affected by the rise of the 'New Right'?
In many ways. Here is one example. Think of the way in which punk took a 'traditionalist' approach to subcultural style, incorporating clothes from all the other subcultures into its sartorial code. Iain Chambers sees this as a sort of ironic commentary on Thatcherism's emphasis on traditional values.

Disappearing in public: the rave scene

The rave scene has been the most important focus for subcultural activity over the last ten years. Like punk before it, it has also led to some major changes in subcultural theory. We shall conclude this chapter by looking at them.

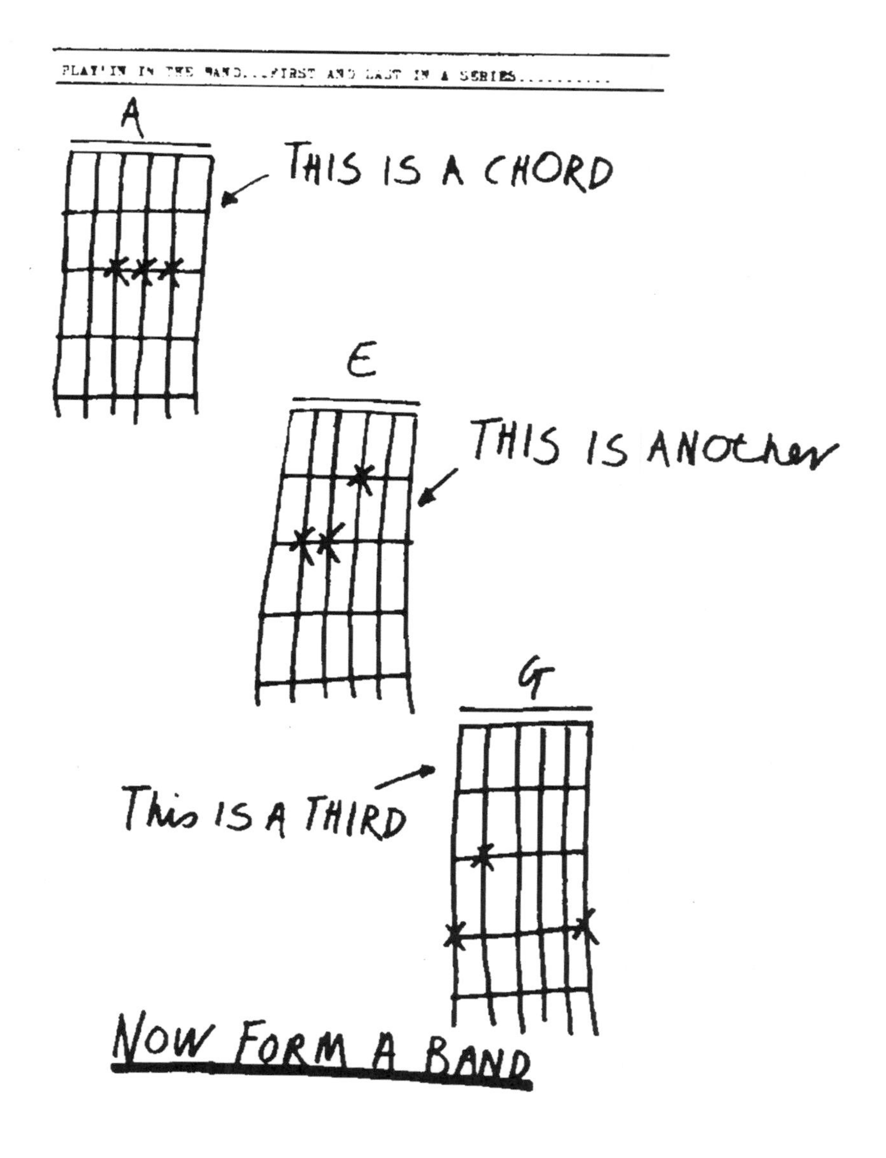

Fig. 6. This famous graphic from the fanzine *Sniffin' Glue* sums up punk's 'do-it-yourself' approach.

Introducing the MIPC

So far, the most suggestive work on rave culture has been done by theorists at the Manchester Institute for Popular Culture (MIPC), based at Manchester Metropolitan University. Among the leading members of this group are Steve Redhead, Antonio Melechi and Hillegonda Rietveld. Their ideas can be found in the influential book *Rave Off: Politics and Deviance in Contemporary Youth Culture*, edited by Steve Redhead. We can examine the work of the MIPC under two headings:

loss of identity
experience of community

Questioning the self

The MIPC believes that the people who participate in the rave scene are likely to experience a crisis of identity. They will begin to feel that their 'sense of self' is being eroded. This will lead them to ask fundamental questions about the sort of people they have become, such as 'who am I?', 'what have I been?' and 'where can I go from here?' Nearly everything about the rave scene tends to produce this effect, but the following factors are especially important:

(a) the eerily 'inhuman' quality of contemporary dance music, with its programmed beats, synthetic textures and disembodied vocals

(b) the effects of the drug Ecstasy

(c) some of the locations in which raves take place, such as abandoned industrial warehouses and fields buried deep in the countryside.

The ecstasy of disappearance

The main consequence of all this is that rave culture rarely has anything to do with personal display. It is clear that dancing, the main activity at raves, is usually a form of showing off. Yet the ravers tend to experience it as a highly introspective activity, because of their sudden preoccupation with issues of personal identity. As they dance, their gaze is likely to be more inwardly-directed than normal. There are even occasions on which they feel that they are disappearing from public view, in spite of their involvement in a ritual which is usually bound up with being watched. This is what Antonio Melechi has in mind when he says that rave culture involves the 'ecstasy of disappearance'.

Why does this idea tend to distinguish the MIPC's work from earlier forms of subcultural theory?
As we have seen, there has often been an emphasis on the 'spectacular' nature of subcultural activity. It has been assumed that subcultures always draw attention to themselves. Yet the MIPC claims that rave culture is more about introspection than personal display.

Why does the MIPC believe that the 'ecstasy of disappearance' is politically significant?
It sees it as a form of symbolic resistance to an increasingly illiberal society in which surveillance plays a major role. Ours is an age in which the state is resorting to highly sophisticated methods of monitoring its citizens. When ravers get the feeling that they are somehow disappearing in public, there is a sense in which they register their dissatisfaction with being permanently 'on display'.

Fusing with the universe
The MIPC now turns its attention to the profound sense of community which people often experience while attending raves. At first sight, this might seem to contradict its earlier emphasis on identity, introspection and 'disappearance'. It isn't immediately clear how someone preoccupied with issues of personal identity would be able to enjoy a 'fusional' relationship with the people around him. Yet the MIPC claims that introspection and community are two sides of the same coin.

The argument goes something like this:

1. If people feel that their identity has been 'thrown into crisis', they will no longer have a clear understanding of the factors which distinguish them from others. It is this which makes possible the sense of community which exists at raves.

2. There is more to this sense of community than feelings of camaraderie. It is common for people at raves to feel that the boundaries between themselves and the world around them have suddenly broken down, so that they experience a feeling of direct contact with other people, the natural world and even the universe as a whole. This is what some writers refer to as **oceanic consciousness**.

3. These feelings of oceanic consciousness are reminiscent of the experience of early childhood, when the child recognises no distinction between itself and the world around it, especially its mother's body.

4. The ability of rave culture to evoke memories of early childhood is reflected in its sartorial code, which incorporates such things as baggy shorts, colourful T-shirts and dummies.

Why does the MIPC believe that the sense of community which people experience at raves is politically significant?
Rave culture emerged at a time when the right-wing administrations of Mrs Thatcher and John Major were disseminating an ideology of extreme individualism. The sense of belonging which lies at the heart of the rave experience is seen as a sort of riposte to this.

Helping you learn

Progress questions

1. How is the CCCS's theory of subcultures guided by the wish to prove that consciousness of class and race are integral to youth culture?

2. How far did the punk movement force cultural theorists to reconsider the principles of subcultural analysis developed by the CCCS during the 1970s?

3. To what extent have recent accounts of rave culture differed from earlier forms of subcultural analysis?

Seminar discussion

1. Many members of subcultures would not be consciously aware that they are doing the things which this chapter says they are doing. Does this mean that subculture theory is invalid?

2. Some people have argued that the age of subcultures is over. Do you agree?

Practical assignment

Think of a subculture which has not been mentioned in this chapter. Read as much as you can about it and try to observe it in action. Can it be analysed in terms of the ideas we have been looking at? Condense your answer to one side of A4.

Study and revision tips

1. Be as clear as you can about the factors which distinguish one group of subculture theorists from another.

2. Try and study some photographs of subcultures. Pay particular attention to aspects of style.

5

Screen

One minute summary – The aim of this chapter is to conclude our survey of Cultural Studies in the 1970s by examining the influence of *Screen*, the most widely-read film journal of the period. *Screen*'s chief contributors were writers such as Colin MacCabe, Stephen Heath, Laura Mulvey and Peter Wollen, who tried to elaborate a 'structuralist' version of Marxist cultural theory. They combined a critique of mainstream cinema with enthusiastic support for experimental directors such as Jean-Luc Godard, who were seen as establishing a powerful alternative to 'Hollywood aesthetics'. *Screen* also published the work of a number of writers critical of its structuralist perspective, notably Richard Dyer. This chapter will help you understand:

- *Screen*'s critique of mainstream cinema
- *Screen*'s account of 'counter cinema'
- Richard Dyer's work on stars

Interpellating the masses

Screen on mainstream cinema

The best way of approaching *Screen*'s work on the cinema is to see it as one of the more pessimistic applications of Marxist cultural theory. It starts from the assumption, central to orthodox Marxism, that culture is part of a 'superstructure' whose purpose is to reinforce support for capitalism, but it then extends the argument in what has sometimes been called a 'structuralist' direction.

Screen's most arresting claim is that the dominant cultural forms make us virtually powerless in the face of capitalist ideology, so that our minds become all but incapable of processing ideas which oppose the *status quo*. Instead of retaining the capacity to think what we like, we are transformed into ideological automatons in a society where it is not human beings who control ideas, but ideas which control human beings.

Screen's argument is that mainstream films are central to this process of ideological indoctrination, whereas certain forms of experimental cinema (see next section) are capable of undermining it. In order to understand its position on mainstream films, we must now look at the following matters:

1. Louis Althusser's theory of ideology.
2. Colin MacCabe's theory of realism in film.
3. Laura Mulvey's account of the representation of women in film.

Summarising Althusser

The foundation of *Screen*'s work on cinema is the theory of ideology worked out by Louis Althusser (1918-1990), the French Marxist philosopher. The following aspects of this theory are especially important:

(a) Ideological discourses are addressed to us by what Althusser calls a 'Unique and central Other Subject', which can roughly be translated as someone (or occasionally something) who occupies a position of special authority. An obvious example is the figure of God in Christian discourse.

(b) The presence of this Other Subject enables ideology to establish an iron grip on our minds.

(c) The process by which the Subject achieves this effect is inherently contradictory. In the first place we feel 'subjected' by it, in the sense that we recognize its authority and feel unwilling to question its word. At the same time, however, there is also a sense in which we choose to *identify* with the Subject, so that our acceptance of its message is rooted in the feelings of personal empowerment which result.

(d) The name which Althusser applies to this process is **interpellation**.

Introducing MacCabe and Mulvey

Let's now examine how *Screen*'s approach to mainstream cinema is influenced by this gloomy doctrine of interpellation. The most important writers in this context are Colin MacCabe and Laura Mulvey. They have each managed to condense their central ideas into a single, highly influential essay:

> *Realism and the Cinema: Notes on Some Brechtian Theses* (MacCabe, 1974)
>
> *Visual Pleasure and Narrative Cinema* (Mulvey, 1976)

Understanding realism

MacCabe argues that mainstream films are chiefly important because they convey an impression of 'realism': they appear to provide us with an extremely accurate portrait of the external world. MacCabe recognises that film is only one of the forms which work in this way, so we will refer here to what he broadly calls the 'realist text' (his other main example is the nineteenth-century novel). MacCabe's central claim is that it is not a text's content which creates an impression of realism, but rather the 'hierarchical' relationship between its various 'discourses'. This often complex argument can be summarised as follows:

1. All realist texts contain two types of discourse. The first – what MacCabe calls the **object language** – encompasses the things said by the characters. The second – what MacCabe calls the **metalanguage** – encompasses the things said by the author. This assumes that the director of a film can broadly be equated with the author of a book, though his means of expression are cinematic rather than verbal.

2. At a very simple level, it is the contrast between the object language and the metalanguage which creates an impression of realism. The object language is associated with characters who

occupy an identifiable position in space and time, but the metalanguage seems wholly unconstrained by any material circumstances. The voice of the author seems so much more 'transparent' than the voices of the characters, creating the illusion that it is especially well-suited to instructing us about the real world.

3. The impression of realism is underscored by the 'hierarchical' relationship between the metalanguage and the object language. One of the central functions of the authorial voice is to criticise, correct and amplify the utterances of the characters, in a manner which reinforces our assumption that it is a privileged form of discourse in possession of special knowledge.

4. Realist texts also employ linear narrative structures. Their events always unfold in a smoothly ordered sequence. By creating a sense of 'seamlessness' at the level of the text, linear narratives cement the belief that there is something equally seamless about the relationship between text and reality.

5. The realist text must therefore be regarded as an extremely powerful means of transmitting the dominant ideology, because its metalanguage is precisely the sort of 'Unique and central Other Subject' which makes interpellation possible.

Comparing Mulvey to MacCabe

How does Mulvey's account of popular film differ from that of MacCabe?
Mulvey agrees with MacCabe that popular films are a powerful source of interpellation, but her analysis focuses more on issues of content than of form. Her central argument is that films are able to interpellate their audience by encouraging them to identify with a strong lead character, who is always male.

How do films manage to achieve this effect?
The twist in Mulvey's argument is that the male hero usually establishes his authority by behaving oppressively towards women, and that two different forms of cinematic 'pleasure' are involved in

this process. The first is that of **scopophilia** (Freud's term for 'pleasure in looking') which occurs when the audience assumes a position of authority in relation to a female character, who is offered up to the camera simply as an 'erotic object' for the benefit of the 'male gaze'. Scopophilia is then translated into the experience of what Mulvey calls **scopophilia in its narcissistic aspect**, which occurs when the audience identifies directly with the strong, independent, unashamedly patriarchal male hero.

So Mulvey's work is an attempt to graft a feminist dimension onto the Althusserian concept of interpellation?
Absolutely. Like all the other *Screen* theorists, Mulvey draws heavily on some very complicated psychoanalytic arguments, most of them derived from the work of the French thinker Jacques Lacan (1905-1980). Once you have mastered the rudiments of *Screen* theory, you should consider exploring these arguments in more detail.

Supporting the avant-garde

Screen on 'counter cinema'

Screen's attack on mainstream films is complemented by its vigorous support for what it sometimes calls **counter cinema**. This term refers to the work of a number of European directors who experimented with avant-garde styles in the 1960s and 1970s. Most of the *Screen* writers identify Jean-Luc Godard (born 1930) as the leading influence on the development of counter cinema, so we will focus on their analysis of his work for the rest of this section.

Godard first came to prominence as a member of the so-called **Nouvelle Vague** (or New Wave) in the late 1950s and early 1960s, when he directed such films as *A Bout de Souffle* (1959) and *Vivre Sa Vie* (1962). Yet *Screen* is more interested in the dauntingly experimental films which came out in the period between 1966 and 1972, when Godard was heavily involved in Marxist (specifically Maoist) politics. These included *La Chinoise* (1967), *Le Gai Savoir* (1968) and *Vent d'Est* (1969).

There are, broadly speaking, two reasons why *Screen* believes that counter cinema is important:

1. In providing an alternative to mainstream aesthetics, it helps to expose the various conventions – realism, linearity and so on – which allow commercial films to successfully convey 'capitalist ideology' to their audience.

2. It has helped to identify the filmic techniques best suited to expressing progressive beliefs.

Introducing Wollen on Godard

In order to understand these claims we will examine the famous essay *Godard and Counter Cinema: Vent d'Est*, written by Peter Wollen in 1972. Some might regard Wollen as a peripheral member of the *Screen* group, but his writings on the avant-garde are infinitely clearer and more systematic than those of MacCabe, Mulvey or Stephen Heath.

Wollen's technique is to base his account of Godard's work on seven distinctions between mainstream and experimental cinema. He presents these in the form of a table, reproduced below. The first column refers to the techniques employed in mainstream films; the second to the techniques employed by Godard.

narrative transitivity	narrative intransitivity
identification	estrangement
transparency	foregrounding
single diegesis	multiple diegesis
closure	aperture
pleasure	unpleasure
fiction	reality

These are the categories of analysis that we will investigate.

Disrupting the storyline

As we saw in the last section, *Screen* has demonstrated how the 'realism' of mainstream films partly depends on their use of linear narratives. Wollen argues that Godard tries to banish this effect of realism by resorting to fragmented storylines. These destroy the viewer's impression that events are unfolding smoothly. This is what he means when he says that Godard swaps 'narrative transitivity' (linearity) with 'narrative intransitivity' (fragmentation).

Among the techniques which contribute to this sense of disruption are the following:

(a) the division of the film into different 'chapters'

(b) the random use of unrelated anecdotes, often on the model of the 'picaresque' novel of the eighteenth century

(c) the deliberate lengthening of digressive material, to the point where it obscures more important aspects of the narrative.

Against identification

The second line of the table refers to Godard's attempts to destroy the conventions that allow audiences to identify with characters. The actors in Godard's films are never endowed with characteristics that would make them seem 'real' to an audience. They are consistently portrayed as alien presences, hence the distinction between 'identification' and 'estrangement'. Godard achieves this effect in a number of ways:

1. He creates a confusing discontinuity between image and sound by failing to match his actors with their real voices.

2. He often introduces real people into films which otherwise depict fictional events.

3. He occasionally allows his actors to speak directly to the audience.

The use of estrangement techniques of this kind is welcomed by *Screen* for at least two reasons:

First, it tends to undermine the sort of interpellative procedures which Laura Mulvey and others have written about (see above, **Comparing Mulvey to MacCabe**), by making it all but impossible for the viewer to identify with a strong central character.

Second, whenever we encounter 'non-naturalistic' forms of acting – acting which makes no attempt to convey an impression of realism –

we are prompted into asking fundamental questions about human behaviour. Instead of empathising with the actor, we ask ourselves such things as 'Why did he do that?', 'Would he really have done that?' and 'Could he have done it differently?' The great value of this sort of response is that it reminds us that there are always alternatives to what we have come to regard as our 'natural' way of doing things. (Note: this argument is derived from the work of the German playwright Bertolt Brecht (1898-1956), whose influence on the *Screen* project is in many ways as great as that of Althusser.)

Foregrounding the process of production

The other central aspect of Godard's work is his attempt to draw our attention to the process by which films are produced. Some of his films contain long sequences which focus on the act of operating a camera, whereas others (notably *Vent d'Est*) use film that has been deliberately marked or scratched. Godard's objective is once again to undermine the illusion of cinematic realism. He reminds us that film involves a complex effort to transform the 'raw materials' of reality into a distinct and 'autonomous' (that is, non-realistic) aesthetic artefact. This is what Wollen means when he says that Godard substitutes 'foregrounding' for 'transparency'.

Summarising the last four lines

The first three lines of Wollen's table correspond to the most important features of Godard's work, but what about the other four?

When Wollen says that Godard uses 'multiple diegesis' rather than 'single diegesis', he means that his films often evoke a series of independent worlds which never overlap. And when he says that Godard substitutes 'aperture' for 'closure', he means the way in which his films are frequently weighed down with references to other works of art until they are all but incomprehensible to the viewer who doesn't share Godard's knowledge. The purpose of these techniques is to convey the impression that art is always a collaborative endeavour, not the product of individual genius.

What about the distinction between 'pleasure' and 'unpleasure'?

It refers to the way in which Godard protests against the irresponsible hedonism of mainstream cinema by stripping his films of any hint of entertainment value.

And, finally, what about the distinction between 'fiction' and 'reality'? In the films which Wollen analyses, Godard seems to be moving away from fiction towards the representation of real events (though not, as should by now be clear, in conventional documentary form). This too can be seen as a dig at mainstream cinema, because it implies that the work of the progressive avant-garde is altogether more truthful (especially at the political level) than that of its 'bourgeois' competitors.

Mainstream films	**Avant-garde films**
Klute (Alan J Pakula)	*Kuhle Wampe* (Bertolt Brecht, Slatan Dudow and Hanns Eisler)
Cathy Come Home (Ken Loach) – described by MacCabe as a a realist film with a radical message	*La Chinoise, Le Gai Savoir* and and *Vent d'est* (Jean-Luc Godard)
Morocco and *Dishonoured* (Josef von Sternberg)	*O Lucky Man!* (Lindsay Anderson) – described by MacCabe as a 'depoliticisation' and 'vulgarisation' of the Brechtian aesthetic
Vertigo, Marnie and *Rear Window* (Alfred Hitchcock) – the films by Sternberg andHitchcock are used by Mulvey in herwork on the representation of women	

Fig. 7. This table lists some of the more important films which the *Screen* theorists have used to illustrate their ideas. Directors' names are in brackets.

Getting your name in lights

Richard Dyer on stars

Most people associate *Screen* with the sort of Althusserian ideas we have just been examining. And yet, when the journal was at the height of its influence in the 1970s, it also helped to establish the reputation of several writers who approached film culture from a different perspective. The most important of these was undoubtedly Richard Dyer, who had earlier been a graduate student at the CCCS. As a means of showing that *Screen* was never monolithic in its mode of analysis, we will conclude this chapter with a brief consideration of Dyer's work.

Analysing stars

Dyer is widely acknowledged to be one of the most versatile figures in the history of Cultural Studies. He has made important contributions to our understanding of gay culture, the utopian dimension of commercial entertainment and the idea of 'whiteness'. But he is best known for his work on stars (especially film stars), the essential principles of which can be found in two books: *Stars* (1979) and *Heavenly Bodies* (1987).

Dyer is especially interested in the relationship between stardom and the idea of individualism. From his more or less Marxist perspective, he sees individualism as one of the central components of capitalist ideology. His basic argument is that although stars usually serve to reinforce support for individualism, there are also times when they can undermine it.

Defining individualism

Since the idea of individualism is obviously central to Dyer's work, perhaps you could explain what he means by it?

Dyer suggests – and he doesn't claim to be original here – that the definition of individualism can be divided into two parts. The first is the idea of 'separateness', which implies that we each possess a personal identity that tends to mark us off from other people. The second is the assertion that we also possess a 'core' of indestructible characteristics which persists throughout our lives.

What is the relevance of the second part of the definition?

An obvious objection to the idea of 'separateness' is the belief that we can be influenced by other people into changing our personalities. Individualism responds to this difficulty by claiming that our most important characteristics are in fact beyond influence, because they are effectively fixed at birth.

Reinforcing individualism

As we have just seen, Dyer argues that stars are an important factor in reinforcing support for individualism. Among other reasons, this is because:

- they privilege the 'private' over the 'public'
- they undergo a series of image changes, yet also appear to maintain a continuous personality.

Privacy in public

One of the most deeply-rooted prejudices in an individualist culture is the belief that the things we do in private are more important than the things we do in public. This is because our private lives allow us to be 'more ourselves' (that is, individual) than would otherwise be possible when we are fulfilling a public role.

Dyer's argument is that stars lend credence to this state of affairs by bringing private matters into the social arena. What usually happens in films, for instance, is that stars who embody a series of private characteristics – sexuality, naturalness, sincerity – are shown operating in a set of distinctly social contexts, such as large towns and cities. This tends to create the impression that private values are somehow taking precedence over the more 'artificial' habits which characterise life in society.

Changing appearances

According to Dyer, stars also play a major role in shoring up the idea of a continuous personality. Most stars are obliged to make frequent changes to their image, both for reasons of publicity and because they have to portray different characters in different films. Yet it is also clear, as Dyer points out, that they tend to remain associated in the public mind with a set of core characteristics assumed to be permanent. We still think of Madonna, for instance, in terms of eroticism, rebellion and female independence, even though she has dramatically altered her 'look' with each new record and film.

Insofar as this aspect of a star's identity implies that we retain a continuous personality in spite of superficial changes, it is seen by Dyer as a powerful support for individualist ideology.

Challenging individualism

But if, as we have just seen, stars seem to exemplify the idea of individualism, how can Dyer argue that there are also occasions on which they are able to undermine it? The following are some of his answers:

(a) We derive our information about stars from a variety of different sources, such as films, newspaper reports, chat shows and gossip. This is what Dyer means when he says that there is an 'intertextual' aspect to the process by which a star's image is produced. Since many of these sources have very different ideas about what a star is 'really like', their combined effect is often to weaken the association between stardom and the idea of coherent selfhood.

(b) Stars would not exist without the media, yet the media is frequently condemned for the way that it intrudes into our private lives. Because stars are therefore associated in some people's minds with the systematic destruction of privacy, their support for individualism can easily come to seem hollow and hypocritical.

(c) Many stars resent the way in which their image is 'manufactured' for public consumption, because they feel that their real personality is not reflected in their work. If it is true (as Dyer believes) that most people have to do jobs which offer no possibility of self-expression, then there is perhaps a sense in which a star's predicament can serve to crystallise wider dissatisfaction with the nature of work in capitalist society.

Helping you learn

Progress questions

1. Assess the influence of Louis Althusser's theory of ideology on *Screen*'s account of mainstream cinema.

2. How is *Screen*'s support for 'counter cinema' related to its wider critique of commercial films?

3. Why does Richard Dyer believe that the existence of film stars serves both to legitimise the ideology of individualism and occasionally to expose its limitations?

Seminar discussion

1. How convincing do you find the doctrine of interpellation?

2. Why have the majority of avant-garde directors failed to achieve widespread popularity?

Practical assignment

Think about the career of your favourite star. Is Richard Dyer right to say that he or she has probably undergone a number of image changes yet still retained a continuous personality? Summarise your answer on a side of A4.

Study and revision tips

1. Suggest to your college film society that they show some of the films of Jean-Luc Godard.

2. Investigate the psychoanalytic ideas on which *Screen* theory is ultimately based.

6

Thatcherism and 'New Times'

One minute summary – There were two developments in the 1980s that prompted Cultural Studies to question its commitment to Marxism. The first was the rise of Thatcherism, which convinced many writers that public opinion had shifted decisively to the right. The second was the growing belief that capitalist society had recently entered 'New Times' (the phrase was coined in the journal *Marxism Today*), such that fundamental change had become impossible to achieve. New Times were said to consist of 'post-Fordism' in the sphere of economics and 'postmodernism' in the sphere of culture. This chapter will help you understand:

- the analysis of Thatcherism
- the idea of post-Fordism
- the idea of postmodernism

Assessing the impact of Thatcherism

When Margaret Thatcher became leader of the Conservative Party in 1975, she inaugurated a lengthy period in which British politics was dominated by the 'New Right'. The rise of the New Right and what came to be known as 'Thatcherism' has been a central theme in Cultural Studies for much of the last 20 years. The most influential writer on Thatcherism has undoubtedly been Stuart Hall. His main ideas can be found in the following sources:

> *Policing the Crisis* (1978), a book he co-wrote with four other members of the CCCS (Charles Critcher, Tony Jefferson, John Clarke and Brian Roberts)
>
> *The Hard Road to Renewal* (1988), a collection of his essays.

Winning public support

Hall's central assertion is that Thatcherism should not be regarded as a passing political trend, but rather as a sustained and extremely successful attempt to shift public opinion towards the right. It can best be described as a form of **authoritarian populism**, in the sense that it has pandered to popular prejudices in order to gain support for its fundamentalist brand of conservatism. Unlike many of her Tory predecessors, with their air of patrician remoteness, Mrs Thatcher has alway seemed deeply attuned to the key preoccupations of the working-class mind.

Responding to crisis

But how can the New Right's campaigning zeal be explained? Hall argues that it was chiefly a response to the 'conjunctural crisis' which began to grip Britain in the late 1960s. This term, first coined by Antonio Gramsci in the 1930s, refers to periods in which several different levels of society are simultaneously thrown into disarray, with the result that the continued existence of the entire social system is suddenly placed in doubt. In *Policing the Crisis*, Hall and his colleagues suggest that the conjunctural crisis of the Thatcher period was caused by a combination of the following factors:

(a) the start of a long economic downturn

(b) the renewed militancy of the trade unions

(c) the threat posed to suburban values by the rise of a 'counter-culture'

(d) the worsening of the situation in Northern Ireland

(e) discontent among ethnic minorities.

The point about a conjunctural crisis, in Hall's opinion, is that it forces 'establishment' groups to redouble their efforts to maintain support for capitalist society. They do this by (1) fighting a 'war of position' in which they appear to offer novel solutions to the whole range of problems that society faces, and (2) striving to establish continuities between their own political agenda and existing elements of popular consciousness. It was the New Right's skill in rising to this challenge which has made it the dominant political force of the last 20 years.

Spreading scare stories

You have said that the New Right was especially good at presenting its case in a way which appealed to ordinary people. Can you give an example?
The most startling assertion made by Hall and his colleagues, specifically in *Policing the Crisis*, is that the core of the New Right's strategy has been a successful attempt to orchestrate a 'moral panic' over crime. The right-wing media, so the argument goes, has joined with politicians in claiming that British society is crumbling under the weight of criminal behaviour, in a deliberate attempt to mislead the public.

But why has the prevalence of moral panics given the New Right a political advantage?
It has made it much easier to advocate an authoritarian approach to politics. And, at the same time, it has allowed the New Right to discredit its political opponents by tarring them with criminal associations. Think, for instance, of the way in which:

1. Conservative discourse on the trade unions has consistently portrayed industrial action as a threat to social order.

2. The New Right has often justified its support for free-market policies by invoking the figure of the 'welfare scrounger'.

3. So-called 'trendy teachers' are said to be creating a new generation of criminals by failing to exert discipline in schools.

But how was the New Right able to create these moral panics in the first place?
The answer, in the opinion of people like Stuart Hall, was that it deliberately exploited anxieties about race by implying that the nation's illusory outbreak of crime had been caused by members of the ethnic minorities. It is this which explains why the New Right

has consistently been portrayed in Cultural Studies as a movement which owes much of its success to racism. Many writers, including Hall and Kobena Mercer, have analysed what they regard as the New Right's racism in considerable detail, noting that:

- It eschews 'biologising' versions of racism – that is, the belief that certain races are inferior to others for biological reasons. It claims instead that people of non-Western origin are condemned to a position of racial inferiority by their historical experience alone.
- It is explicitly populist in tone, insisting that most ordinary people naturally hold 'muscular' views on race which the media has chosen to suppress.
- It is linked to a broader attempt to popularise a 'good myth' about Britain's imperial history, the main purpose of which is to ease despair over the loss of empire by claiming that it was never central to national consciousness in the first place.

Summarising the effects of Thatcherism

The belief that Thatcherism had caused a significant 'break to the right' was to have a major impact on the politics of Cultural Studies. Not least, it convinced many scholars that their commitment to Marxism was becoming increasingly untenable. The shift away from Marxism was reinforced later in the 1980s, when it was claimed that capitalist society had now entered 'New Times' which made fundamental change even more unlikely. It is to the debate on New Times that we now turn.

Understanding 'New Times'

The debate about 'New Times' was launched by the journal *Marxism Today* towards the end of 1988. Among its key participants were writers from a broad range of academic subjects, including Cultural Studies (Stuart Hall, Dick Hebdige, Rosalind Brunt), Political Theory (Tom Nairn, Paul Hirst) and History (Gareth

Stedman Jones, Gwyn Alf Williams). The central premise of the debate was that most Western societies have recently entered a new stage of their development, characterised by:

- the growth of a **post-Fordist** mode of organising the capitalist economy
- the emergence of **postmodernism** as a distinctive cultural form.

Neither of these propositions was new, but they were both to acquire a special influence in Cultural Studies as a result of being singled out for debate. Since postmodernism is often seen as having its origins in the growth of post-Fordism, we need to make a brief detour through economics before returning to the cultural aspects of New Times.

Itemising post-Fordism

The term post-Fordism implies that most Western economies have now moved beyond the 'Fordist' stage of their development, which is said to have occurred in the period between 1920 and 1970 (these dates are highly approximate). Named after the American car manufacturer Henry Ford (1863–1947), the central feature of Fordism was the mass production of standardised goods by very large companies, most of them organised on a national basis. It was common for Fordist companies to (1) employ an exclusively male workforce, (2) use 'assembly-line' techniques of production, and (3) favour a hierarchical and centralised style of management. When Ford announced that 'people can have the Model T in any colour – so long as it's black', he summed up the mood of sameness and inflexibility which pervaded the entire system.

So how does post-Fordism differ from its predecessor? In his essay *The Meaning of New Times*, Stuart Hall suggests that it has nine distinguishing characteristics, which can be summarised as follows:

- First, computers and other forms of information technology have moved to the centre of economic life, replacing the heavy industry which predominated during the Fordist period.

- Second, the labour process is now more 'flexible, specialised and decentralised'.

- Third, it is no longer common for individual companies to oversee all aspects of production, because many tasks are now 'hived off' to external sources.

- Fourth, each sector of the market has become highly segmented, in the sense that a bewildering variety of 'differentiated' products is increasingly being targeted at specific groups of consumers.

- Fifth, the size of the industrial working class has been substantially reduced, while the size of the 'service and white-collar classes' has greatly increased.

- Sixth, the workforce now contains a large number of women as well as members of the ethnic minorities, many of them doing part-time jobs.

- Seventh, the most important companies are now organised on a 'multinational' basis.

- Eighth, the financial system has become increasingly 'globalised'.

- Ninth, there is a wide division between the two-thirds of the population whom the system maintains in a state of affluence, and the one-third who live in less comfortable circumstances.

Explaining postmodernism

Most writers who contributed to the New Times debate were in broad agreement about the characteristics of post-Fordism, but there was nothing approaching unanimity when it came to postmodernism. There has, indeed, been such a proliferation of theories about postmodernism that we can only examine some of them here.

When British writers have explored this aspect of New Times, they have tended to draw extensively on the work of such foreign theorists as Jean-Francois Lyotard, Jean Baudrillard and Fredric Jameson. In a sense, therefore, this section is concerned less with British Cultural Studies than with the international debate about postmodernism, which writers like Hall and Hebdige have simply popularised for the benefit of a British readership. As such, we will be concentrating on the argument that postmodern culture involves:

(a) a rejection of the 'metanarratives' of the modern period

(b) a weakening sense of history

(c) a feeling of disorientation in 'hyperspace'

(d) the emergence of a 'hyper-real' network of images.

Rejecting metanarratives

In his book *The Postmodern Condition* (1979), the French writer Jean-Francois Lyotard argues that the key characteristic of postmodern culture is its rejection of the 'metanarratives' which predominated in Western societies during the modern period (the eighteenth century onwards).

A metanarrative can be defined as any social theory which possesses the following features:

(a) the claim to have achieved perfect or near-perfect knowledge about the way that society works, usually by taking a 'totalising' perspective on social affairs. When we say that a metanarrative is totalising, we mean that it treats a particular institution or practice as the determining influence over all other aspects of the social structure. As an example, think of how Marxism identifies the economy as the central institution in society, and how it then tends to treat everything else – politics, culture, ideology etc – as an 'expression' of economic affairs.

(b) the claim that it points the way towards universal liberation, in the sense of telling us what we ought to do if we wish to establish a society in which *everyone* will lead a happy, creative and fulfilling life.

Lyotard's point is that metanarratives were at the heart of the modern outlook, whereas postmodern societies are incapable of taking them seriously. Among the most important metanarratives of the modern period were liberalism, Marxism, the philosophy of Hegel, and certain forms of Christianity.

Explaining metanarratives

How does Lyotard explain the prevalence of metanarratives in modern societies?

His central point is that the proliferation of metanarratives was closely related to the birth of modern science. In the modern period, so the argument goes, science was bound up with two assumptions:

1. It could provide humanity with perfect knowledge of the physical universe.

2. Its practical consequences made it a powerful instrument of human liberation.

And yet it was still necessary for the sciences to find some means of 'legitimising' themselves (making themselves acceptable), because many people regarded scientific knowledge as inherently threatening and disruptive. This was achieved, in Lyotard's opinion, by trying to ensure that the assumptions which surrounded science – especially those of perfect knowledge and human liberation – were reflected in all other areas of human activity, such as politics, culture and religion. Hence the birth of the metanarratives.

So why, in postmodern societies, do the metanarratives no longer command our allegiance?

This is another matter which can only be explained by invoking the development of science. Lyotard argues that our perception of science has undergone a fundamental change in the period since 1945. We no longer believe that it gives us perfect or even reliable knowledge about the physical universe, and we have come to think of it as an alien force over which we have too little control. The point about postmodern culture follows on logically from these assumptions. If the older model of science has now largely disappeared, then it is clear that the metanarratives by which it legitimised itself have also outlived their usefulness.

But why has our perception of science changed so fundamentally? Lyotard proposes a number of reasons for science's changing status, including the following:

(a) The rise of computerisation has ensured that scientific knowledge is now as much a product of artificial as of human intelligence.

(b) Scientific theories have emerged which emphasise the unpredictability of the physical universe (chaos theory and the uncertainty principle, for instance).

(c) Scientific knowledge occupies a central position in the 'information economy'. In other words it is frequently sold for profit on the free market.

(d) Scientific knowledge is now evaluated less by cognitive criteria ('is it true?') than by the criterion of performativity ('does it work?').

Forgetting history

Lyotard's point about metanarratives is echoed by the various writers who claim that postmodern societies display a weakening sense of history. This argument presupposes that an awareness of historical change has been central to Western culture since the advent of the modern age. It is assumed, in other words, that modern consciousness has been shaped by the recognition that society is in a state of permanent transformation. The prospect of change has usually been viewed in one of two ways. Many people have believed in the inevitability of progress, whereas others have convinced themselves that society is on the verge of imminent collapse.

But according to writers like Jean Baudrillard and Fredric Jameson (the former is a French philosopher, the latter an American literary theorist), it is precisely this sort of historical awareness that has been eliminated from postmodern culture. The assumption now is that we all live in what is sometimes called a 'permanent present', convinced that the existing structure of society is destined to last forever. Among the various explanations which have been offered for this state of affairs, two are worth emphasising:

1. Some writers have argued, perhaps rather paradoxically, that our weakened sense of history has been caused by the accelerating pace of change in contemporary society. At a time of increased market segmentation (see above, **Itemising post-Fordism**), fashions alter with bewildering speed and working practices are continually being transformed. The prospect of rapid change can then seem so disorientating that people retreat into a permanent present as a means of self-protection.

2. Baudrillard, by contrast, focuses more closely on the role of the media. Since the broadcast media can now report on important events as soon as they occur, it often bombards its audience with information that is manifestly false, contradictory and impossible to piece together into a coherent whole. The main consequence is that we lose the ability to even *understand* world affairs, and relinquish any sense that history is being pushed forward by important political developments.

Losing our way

Some writers claim that postmodern culture has had as big an impact on our perception of space as on our sense of time. This theme has been explored in particular detail by Fredric Jameson. He argues that our perception of space is now characterised by profound feelings of disorientation. Instead of moving easily through a world whose 'spatial coordinates' are familiar, we find that we are increasingly uncertain of our surroundings and stunted in our movements. The root of the problem, in Jameson's opinion, is that capitalism has now extended across the entire face of the globe, with the result that we can no longer fix an accurate mental picture of the system which governs our lives. Space has given way to 'hyperspace'.

Responding to hyper-reality

This emphasis on disorientation is taken to an extreme in the work of Jean Baudrillard, whose ideas about postmodernism and history we have already examined (see above, **Forgetting history**). Baudrillard's chief concern is with the impact of the vast network of images which now stares out at us from television screens, advertising hoardings, computer terminals and a host of other sources. He argues that these images, to which he gives the collective title of 'hyper-reality', are distinguished by the following characteristics:

(a) They are **ubiquitous**. They dominate both our private lives (the television in the lounge) as well as our public spaces (advertisements in the high street).

(b) They are **non-referential**. They constitute a sort of parallel universe which is quite different from the 'real world' that exists alongside it.

(c) They are **intertextual**. They bind themselves together into a single loop by continually referring to each other.

Baudrillard believes that the rise of this hyper-real order has caused a major cultural catastrophe. He describes the postmodern age as one of accelerated decline, in which most people have succumbed to mental disorder and society itself is on the verge of grinding to a halt. This, he argues, is because our obsession with images has had the following effects, among many others:

(1) It has increased the level of narcissistic personality disorders

If it is true, as Baudrillard claims, that the images which surround us bear 'no relation to any reality whatever', then there is clearly a sense in which we all live in two different world simultaneously. This explains what Baudrillard regards as the most startling feature of postmodern culture – our widespread habit of projecting media images onto the world around us. Instead of accepting that the hyper-real order is one of 'simulation' and not 'reflection', we insist on behaving as if everyday realities are no different from the imaginary worlds which we encounter on television or at the cinema. A powerful example, cited in most introductory works on Baudrillard, would be the thousands of people who write letters of advice to the characters in soap operas, believing that they really exist.

Baudrillard argues that this habit causes most people to experience symptoms of 'narcissism', in the clinical sense of being unable to distinguish between 'self' and 'other'. Because of our obsession with projecting what is essentially the product of the human imagination (that is, the images which surround us) onto our everyday circumstances, we fall prey to the dangerous delusion that the external world is simply an extension of our own thoughts.

(2) It has caused an epidemic of schizophrenia

The emphasis on mental disorder is also evident in Baudrillard's extraordinary remarks about the prevalence of schizophrenia in contemporary society. His starting point here is the argument that the old distinction between public and private has now been virtually destroyed, not least because of the effects of television. By constantly beaming information about the wider world into our domestic spaces, television has forced us to conceive of external reality as a sort of unwanted intruder – tenacious, unpleasant, never leaving us alone in its bid for our attention. The consequence, in Baudrillard's opinion, is that the world around us seems to acquire a nightmarish intensity, hurting our eyes with its 'absolute proximity'. Psychiatrists tell us that this is one of the main perceptual disorders which characterise schizophrenia.

Moving away from Marxism

But why has the emergence of New Times caused Cultural Studies to distance itself from Marxism?

Because the combined effect of post-Fordism and postmodernism has been to undermine the belief that capitalist society is susceptible to thorough-going change. This is for the following reasons, among others:

'Modern' society	'New Times'
heavy industry	computers
homogeneous workforce	fragmented workforce
unified market	'market segmentation'
national monopolies	multinational companies
belief in universal liberation	'an incredulity towards all metanarratives' (Lyotard)
unified self	fragmented or 'decentred' self
historical consciousness	permanent present
command of space	hyperspace
reality	hyper-reality

Fig. 8. This chart allows you to compare the key features of New Times to those of the 'modern' society which preceded them.

1. The collapse of the metanarratives has destroyed the idea of universal liberation.

2. The destruction of historical consciousness has blinded us to the existence of political alternatives.

3. The recomposition of the workforce (see points two, three, five and six in our description of post-Fordism) has undermined the unity of the working class.

4. The rise of market segmentation has created a bewilderingly diverse culture.

5. The 'globalisation' of the economy has reduced the power of the nation state.

6. The emergence of widespread forms of disorientation (see **Losing our way** and **Responding to hyper-reality**) has ensured that personal survival is now more of a priority than collective action.

Helping you learn

Progress questions

1. What do you understand by the claim that Thatcherism represented a form of 'authoritarian populism'?

2. Why did the emergence of 'New Times' cause many scholars in Cultural Studies to question their commitment to Marxism?

3. What do you regard as the central features of postmodern culture?

Seminar discussion

1. Would you agree that British society has recently experienced a 'moral panic' over crime?

2. Is it true that we no longer believe in metanarratives?

Practical assignment

Ask a cross section of your fellow students about their hopes for Britain's future. Do their responses bear out the claim that we have now arrived at the 'end of history'?

Study and revision tips

1. Read some more about the historical background to the rise of the New Right.

2. Try and be clear about the ways that post-Fordism and postmodernism are related.

7

Cultural Populism

One minute summary – Towards the end of the 1980s an element of 'cultural populism' began to appear in Cultural Studies, notably in the work of John Fiske and Paul Willis. Its main characteristic was a sort of unrestrained enthusiasm about popular culture, rooted in the conviction that there is something inherently creative and progressive in the way that ordinary people respond to commercial texts. Though similar to culturalism (see Chapters 3 and 4), cultural populism was also far more optimistic. The culturalists had merely argued that popular culture can *occasionally* be the site of political resistance, whereas writers like Fiske and Willis seemed to assume that it nearly always is. This chapter will help you understand:

- the ideas of John Fiske
- the ideas of Paul Willis
- some of the key criticisms of cultural populism

Evading and producing

The ideas of John Fiske

John Fiske became an important figure in Cultural Studies in the late 1970s, long before his turn towards cultural populism. It is only his more recent work that will be of interest to us in this chapter, especially his two books *Understanding Popular Culture* and *Reading the Popular* (both published in 1989). The argument which Fiske develops in these books can be summarised as follows:

(1) Most popular texts aim to reinforce the *status quo*, but it is rare for their meanings to be passively absorbed. It is far more common for ordinary people (or just 'the people', as Fiske likes to call them) to respond 'creatively' to the texts which they

encounter, consciously reshaping them with a view to expressing progressive meanings.

(2) This approach to texts tends to be divided into two stages. The first is that of **evasion**, whereby the people show their dislike of a text's ideology by subjecting it to various forms of 'offensive' behaviour. Common examples of evasion would be swearing at the television, screwing up a newspaper or expressing violent disbelief at the content of an advertisement.

(3) Acts of evasion produce a burst of primitive energy that prepares the way for the next stage of oppositional decoding, which Fiske calls **productivity**. Productivity occurs when a text is reordered to express alternative meanings, either literally or at the level of the imagination.

As an example of what Fiske means by evasion and productivity, put yourself in the position of an impoverished student watching television in a poky Hall of Residence. There is an item on the news which shows a leading politician, possibly the Secretary of State for Education, being driven to the House of Commons to deliver a controversial speech announcing cutbacks in funding for colleges and universities. Having roused yourself to hurl some choice words of abuse at the screen (this is the moment of evasion), you are now sufficiently fired up to indulge in a mischievous political fantasy. You imagine that once the politician has finished his speech, he goes outside to find that his government chauffeur has driven off in disgust. He has no choice but to go to the tube station, where he discovers that he doesn't have enough money to buy a ticket home. This little act of productivity, in which you cheekily alter the meanings of the programme you've just been watching, is your way of fighting back against the powerful people whose decisions affect your life.

Continuing the argument

In order to extend our understanding of Fiske's idea of popular creativity, we must now examine the following aspects of his work:

(a) his account of the 'carnivalesque' aspects of popular texts

(b) his description of the process of productivity

(c) his conception of the 'producerly' nature of popular texts.

Residues of carnival

As we have just seen, Fiske maintains that evasion is ultimately a mark of hostility towards a text's dominant meanings. At the same time, however, he claims that the majority of popular texts also exhibit a number of 'carnivalesque' characteristics, which tend to reinforce the evasive response whenever it occurs. His argument at this point is deeply influenced by the work of Mikhail Bakhtin (1895–1975), the Russian literary theorist and philosopher of language. Bakhtin was especially interested in the popular carnivals which were held throughout Europe in the mediaeval and early-modern periods, and whose main purpose was to allow the 'lower orders' to briefly indulge their baser appetites in an orgy of drunkenness, promiscuity, blasphemy and social dissent. He argued that carnivals have not only exercised a massive influence on elite culture (as in the work of Rabelais, Shakespeare and Dostoevsky), but that their traces can also be detected in the popular culture of the present.

Following Bakhtin's lead, Fiske argues that there are at least three ways in which modern popular texts exhibit carnivalesque characteristics:

1. Carnivals often featured 'comic compositions' in which symbolic humiliation was inflicted on priests, landowners and other members of the social elite. Fiske observes that a strain of primitive anti-elitism is still a central feature of popular texts, though it is now expressed less virulently.

2. One of the most effective methods of satirizing the elite was to portray them in grotesque form, though Bakhtin also notes that there were many other ways in which displays of physical grotesquerie were integrated into the 'popular spectacles' which occurred at carnivals. Fiske points out that an emphasis on the

grotesque has survived in many forms of popular entertainment, especially wrestling.

3. It was common for the everyday prohibition on bad language to be suspended while carnivals were taking place, with the result that the air would suddenly become thick with what Fiske calls 'curses, oaths and popular blazons'. This delight in 'billingsgate' is the other obvious way in which modern culture reflects the tradition of carnivalesque misbehaviour.

Understanding carnival: some final questions

Why does Fiske believe that the carnivalesque aspects of popular texts tend to encourage evasion?
By putting a premium on irreverence towards the elite, enjoyment of physical excess and forthright methods of self-expression, carnivalesque culture is clearly all of a piece with the spirit of primitive rebellion which fuels acts of evasion.

Are there any other reasons why Fiske values the carnivalesque dimension of popular texts?
Yes. He believes that there are various ways in which it tends to have progressive consequences, quite apart from its links with evasion. He points out, for instance, that:

1. It is usually men rather than women who are represented in grotesque form (note the feminist implications of this argument).

2. There is something deeply egalitarian about displays of grotesquerie, in the sense that none of us can stand on our dignity when reminded of our bodily limitations.

3. Carnivalesque activities induce feelings of bliss or 'jouissance' which have a transformative effect on our sense of personal identity (the term jouissance is borrowed by Fiske from the French theorist Roland Barthes).

Producing texts of our own

Though Fiske recognises that evasion is important in itself, his central emphasis is on the way that it encourages audiences to engage in a more profound form of oppositional decoding, which he calls productivity. As we have already seen, productivity occurs when a text is actively rearranged (either literally or at the level of the imagination) to express progressive meanings. But what are the precise characteristics of a productive reading? And what sort of features must a text exhibit if this form of 'popular creativity' is to flourish? These are the questions we must now answer.

Defining productivity

Having emphasised that the ultimate purpose of productivity is to graft progressive meanings onto mainstream texts, Fiske argues that most productive readings will also display the following characteristics:

(a) they will adopt a 'micropolitical' approach to social problems

(b) they will be both 'relevant' and 'functional'

(c) their dominant emotional tone will be one of embarrassment.

Finding small-scale solutions

When Fiske says that the majority of productive readings are 'micropolitical', he means that they tend to focus on small-scale acts of resistance, rather than on large-scale or 'macropolitical' attempts to transform the system as a whole. This is why he argues that it is more accurate to regard productivity as 'progressive' rather than 'radical'.

Being practical

Apart from being micropolitical, Fiske also insists that productive readings are likely to be 'relevant' and 'functional', in the sense that they will encourage forms of resistance that can easily be put into practice in everyday situations. It is interesting to compare this argument with the widespread conviction that popular culture is essentially a site of 'escapist' pleasures, whose main effect is to weaken people's ability to cope in the real world.

Feeling embarrassed
According to Fiske, the main feeling which people experience during acts of productivity is one of mild embarrassment, because they know that they are flouting the values of established society. The emotional structure of popular creativity is therefore characterised by a violent contrast between the anger of evasion and the embarrassment of productivity.

Encouraging productivity

Fiske's argument culminates in the assertion that the majority of popular texts actually *encourage* the habit of productivity, by exhibiting a number of what he calls 'producerly' characteristics (that is, characteristics whose main effect is to stimulate active decodings). This idea is summarised in the following table, which lists both the producerly characteristics which Fiske finds most important (column one) and the forms of productivity to which they allegedly give rise (column two).

Producerly characteristics	**Associated forms of productivity**
Polysemy	encourages the conviction that there is nothing inviolate about a text's dominant meanings
Textual poverty (that is, lack of attention to detail in popular texts)	forces the audience to use its imagination to 'fill in' textual gaps
Excess	fosters a critical perspective on reality by implying that 'normal' life is dull and uninteresting
Intertextuality	legitimises the practice of 'bringing in' outside material to modify a text's meanings

Fig. 9. Fiske's list of producerly characteristics and productivity.

Practising symbolic creativity: the ideas of Paul Willis

The other writer who helped to pioneer the shift towards cultural populism was Paul Willis, whose main ideas are contained in the two books which he published on the same day in 1990. The aim of *Moving Culture* and *Common Culture* (the first is an introductory version of the second) is to summarise the results of an ethnographic investigation into the 'cultural activities of young people', carried out at the behest of the Gulbenkian Foundation in the late 1980s. (It is worth noting immediately that Willis is writing in these books about people under the age of 23, though he claims that many of his arguments can be extended to other age groups as well.)

Summarising the argument

On the basis of his research (much of it undertaken with other leading figures in Cultural Studies, such as Angela McRobbie, Kobena Mercer and Graham Murdock), Willis developed a version of cultural populism which can be summarised as follows:

(1) The majority of young people employ a form of **symbolic creativity** when responding to commercial culture. Far from being the victims of an entertainment industry which ruthlessly exploits them, they are skilled at using its products in order to reshape their identities, dramatise their actions and lend aesthetic lustre to their everyday circumstances. It is important to be clear about the ways in which Willis differs from Fiske. Whereas Fiske tends to concentrate on the ideology of popular texts, Willis is more interested in what we might call their 'existential' implications – that is to say, in their ability to transform the inner lives of the people who encounter them. Think, for instance, of the following very common examples of symbolic creativity:

- the way that popular songs are often used to intensify personal relationships
- the way that many young people try to model themselves on their favourite stars
- the way that many viewers make sense of their own lives by identifying with fictional characters on the television.

(2) The sense of 'control' which people acquire through symbolic creativity is a precondition of successful political action.

(3) The rise of popular creativity has been accompanied by a collapse in the influence of the 'traditional' arts, which now seem less relevant than ever to the majority of ordinary people. This is not because of any intrinsic deficiencies in high culture itself, but rather because the contexts in which it is encountered have become remote and deadening.

(4) It is necessary to reformulate cultural policy in the light of the foregoing arguments. We must recognise, in particular, that the main aim of government policy should be to strengthen existing forms of popular creativity, not to promote the high arts.

Our task in the rest of this section is to expand on this summary by asking the following questions:

1. Why does Willis believe that symbolic creativity is now a central feature of popular culture?

2. Why does he believe that the influence of the traditional arts has declined?

3. What are his proposals in the field of cultural policy?

Explaining symbolic creativity

Although he recognises that symbolic creativity has always been a feature of popular culture, Willis also argues that it has only become a majority practice over the course of the last few decades. But why should this be so? There are, in Willis's opinion, at least three explanations:

(a) at the most basic level, the flowering of symbolic creativity is obviously linked to the post-war expansion of the culture industries, which are now the dominant influence on our everyday lives. If popular texts have become a widespread source of what Willis calls 'aesthetic realisation', then part of the explanation is simply that they are more readily available than at any time in the past

(b) the economies of most Western societies have undergone a sustained process of 'modernisation' in the period since 1945, with a consequent increase in poorly paid, unskilled and unfulfilling forms of employment. The growth of a vibrant popular culture has been the main way in which ordinary people have compensated for the absence of creative possibilities in their working lives

(c) in a nod to postmodern theory (see Chapter 6), Willis argues that ours is an age of weakening subjectivity, in which the majority of people are plagued by the feeling that it is impossible to maintain a stable sense of self in the face of rapid and continuous change. From this perspective, symbolic creativity is best understood as an attempt to stabilise the self by establishing a strong alternative identity.

Rejecting the arts

Why does Willis believe that the majority of people now regard the traditional arts as completely irrelevant?

The central point, as we have already said, is not that there is anything wrong with the arts themselves, but rather that the assumptions which surround them have become inherently alienating. The most damaging assumption of all is that it is only possible for people to appreciate the arts if they are naturally gifted.

What's wrong with that?

It ensures that most of us feel excluded from high culture by birth alone. At the same time, however, Willis is also worried by the current state of arts education. He believes that the majority of people who study the arts end up 'bored through and through' with them, because their sensibility has been corrupted by the aesthetic assumptions which are currently disseminated in schools and colleges.

What assumptions are those?
First, that it is more important to appreciate form than to analyse content; second, that it is necessary to arrange works of art in strictly-defined hierarchies or 'canons'; third, that it is essential to cultivate an attitude of self-denial if aesthetic understanding is to be achieved. The problem with these assumptions, in Willis's opinion, is that they make the arts seem bloodless and remote from everyday life, in a process which he dubs 'hyperinstitutionalisation'.

Rethinking cultural policy

The final part of Willis's project is his attempt to outline a new approach to cultural policy, based on his understanding of the role of symbolic creativity in the lives of young people. His starting point, as we have already seen, is the belief that the government should no longer place such emphasis on promoting high culture, but should strive instead to strengthen existing forms of popular creativity. He suggests five main areas in which this could begin:

- First, it is necessary to find a method of subsidising the cultural activities of young people, perhaps by establishing a network of 'cultural exchanges' at the local level.

- Second, the government must be willing to supplement the output of the culture industries by doing two things: (1) taking responsibility for the continued availability of popular texts which are no longer produced commercially, and (2) engaging in a form of short-term 'market testing' by releasing the work of new artists who have yet to secure commercial support.

- Third, since it is now clear that symbolic creativity tends to flourish in informal settings, steps should be taken to ensure that cultural institutions are made to seem less forbidding to the public.

- Fourth, structures should be established to allow young people to exercise a direct influence over the decisions of the culture industries.

- Fifth, the cultural activities of young people should be more broadly reflected in education and training, especially in the following ways: (1) the study of popular culture should be given a prominent role in the arts curriculum; (2) universities and other institutions of higher education should put their 'cultural resources' at the disposal of the entire community; and (3) training schemes should be established in creative activities such as popular music, video and film, not least because these are a rich source of 'transferable skills'.

Attacking cultural populism

Cultural populism has come under vigorous attack from a number of writers, including Jim McGuigan, Paul Willemen and Simon Frith. There is no space here in which to summarise their entire critique of people like Fiske and Willis, but the following arguments are among the most frequently heard:

(a) Cultural populism can in some respects be regarded as a distant cousin of free-market ideology, especially in the way that it constantly emphasises the culture industry's sensitivity to consumer needs.

(b) It is wrong for writers like Fiske and Willis, who have both benefited from an extensive education, to reinforce the cultural deprivation suffered by many ordinary people by telling them that commercial culture is more important than the high arts.

(c) Cultural populism is ultimately a symptom of political defeat (specifically the collapse of Marxism), because it tries to compensate for the absence of radicalism in social affairs by pretending that the people's oppositional instincts have now taken root in the sphere of culture.

Helping you learn

Progress questions

1. What does John Fiske mean when he says that audiences employ the strategies of 'evasion' and 'productivity' when responding to the dominant meanings contained in popular texts?

2. Relate Paul Willis's writings on cultural policy to his understanding of the role of 'symbolic creativity' in the lives of young people.

3. '. . . an unquestioning endorsement of the "popular" is downright hypocritical on the part of critics who are themselves well endowed with cultural capital and possess privileged access to both "high" and "popular" culture' (Jim McGuigan, summarising the argument of Jostein Gripsrud). Is this a fair comment on the work of the cultural populists?

Seminar discussion

1. Would you agree that there is a 'carnivalesque' dimension to popular texts?

2. Should the cultural activities of young people be subsidised by the government?

Practical assignment

Write an account of the way that symbolic creativity has affected your own life.

Study and revision tips

1. Read some more about Bakhtin's theory of carnival.

2. Make sure that you are able to distinguish Fiske's version of cultural populism from that of Willis.

8

New Social Movements

One minute summary – The politics of Cultural Studies is now dominated by what are sometimes called the 'new social movements', especially the feminist, anti-racist and gay liberation movements. We will concentrate in this chapter on work produced from a feminist perspective. Some feminist writers have taken a critical perspective on existing work in Cultural Studies, condemning it for its unconscious sexism. But others have developed entirely new forms of cultural analysis, based on the need both to defend women's culture and to encourage a specifically feminist approach to cultural politics. This chapter will help you understand:

- the feminist critique of existing work in Cultural Studies
- the feminist defence of so-called 'women's genres'
- the idea of a feminist intervention in contemporary culture

Criticising Cultural Studies

There is a sense in which feminism's relationship with Cultural Studies has always been an uneasy one, even though it is now one of the most influential ideologies in the field. Many feminist writers have argued that Cultural Studies tends to betray a 'sexist' or 'patriarchal' bias, both in its approach to cultural analysis and in the way that it is organised as a subject. These points were first raised back in the 1970s by the Women's Study Group at the CCCS, specifically in its path-breaking volume *Women Take Issue* (1978).

Reconsidering the New Left

The best way of approaching the feminist critique of Cultural Studies is to examine Morag Schiach's influential essay *Feminism and Popular Culture* (1991), which briskly surveys the whole history of the subject in the matter of a few pages. Schiach begins with the emergence of Cultural Studies in the 1950s (see Chapter 2 of the present study), claiming that the work of early New Leftists such as Raymond Williams, Richard Hoggart and EP Thompson should be regarded as unconsciously patriarchal for the following reasons:

1. When it tried to promote a common culture based on the distinctive values of working-class life, it ignored the way that 'traditional' working-class communities were organised according to a gendered division of labour (husbands at work, wives at home) that was extremely oppressive to women.

2. When it called for high culture to be integrated into the nation's 'common inheritance', it overlooked the way that men have often used canonical texts in order to legitimise their position of dominance.

3. When it condemned commercial culture for its trashiness and vulgarity, it tended to reinforce the assumption that these qualities are chiefly enjoyed by women.

Emphasising public resistance

Schiach insists that the New Left's patriarchal outlook was inherited by many of the writers who have dominated Cultural Studies over the last 30 years. Surveying the work of the CCCS in the 1970s, she reminds us that the Centre's primary interest was in forms of *collective* resistance to capitalist society, especially in the context of subculture studies (see Chapter 4). The problem with this approach, she argues, is that it downgraded the majority of cultural activities which are important to women, since these tend to be private rather than public. It was not that women were disparaged, more that they were ignored because of their perceived lack of political engagement.

Shiach's comments on subculture theory are based on the work of Angela McRobbie, which is worth glancing at here before we return to *Feminism and Popular Culture*. In a number of important essays, one of them co-written with Jenny Garber, McRobbie has argued that feminists have the following reasons to be suspicious of subcultures and orthodox subculture theory:

1. The subcultural technique of 'bricolage' tends to be deeply alienating to most women, who find it redolent of male aggression.

2. The stylistic resources which subcultures draw on are often highly 'masculinist', in the sense of being closely associated with the expression of male power (think, for instance, of the teddy boys' appropriation of Edwardian fashions or the skinheads' liking for the industrial styles of the pre-war period).

3. Many forms of 'symbolic resistance' involve the expression of hostility towards women.

4. It is only men who usually feel comfortable with the forms of public display which lie at the heart of subcultural activity.

Assessing the feminist response

At the end of her essay, Schiach turns her attention towards the role of the feminist movement in Cultural Studies. Her conclusion, somewhat surprisingly, is that although much of the work which feminist writers have produced is extremely valuable, its overall effect has been to reinforce the marginal position of women in Cultural Studies as a whole. This is because it has allegedly focused on a narrow range of topics, such as the cultural significance of 'female genres' like the soap opera and romance novel, which have served only to emphasise women's links to the purely *private* sphere of 'pleasure and consumption'. This argument provides us with a good cue to proceed to the next section.

Defending 'women's genres'

It is clear that most popular forms associated chiefly with women are still held in very low esteem. If we think of such 'women's genres' as the soap opera, the romance novel or the 'weepie', we find that two accusations tend to be regularly levelled against them:

(a) They are said to be aesthetically substandard, usually on the grounds that they promote a form of 'escapism' which is held to be demeaning.

(b) They are said to reduce their audience (that is, women) to a state of something approaching moronic passivity.

The perceived awfulness of women's genres has gone a long way towards reinforcing the assumption that women are both culturally and intellectually inferior to men. It is not surprising, therefore, that one of the key objectives of feminist Cultural Studies has been to rescue women's genres from the disdain in which they are currently held. In response to the two arguments that we have just summarised, many feminist scholars have claimed that:

1. Women's genres are far more complex and aesthetically satisfying than is usually recognised.

2. It is common for the female audience to respond to women's genres in highly creative and intelligent ways.

Anticipating utopia

Most of the really influential work on the first of these claims has been produced by non-British writers such as Tania Modleski (from the USA) and Ien Ang (from Holland). Both have written extensively on the 'melodramatic' dimension of soap operas.

But there are several British writers who also need to be considered. If we look, for instance, at Christine Geraghty's book *Women and Soap Opera* (1991), we find an ingenious argument against the assertion that all women's genres are blandly escapist. Geraghty's claim is that women's genres are not so much escapist as inspiringly *utopian*, in the sense that they provide us with a glimpse of an ideal world.

Following the lead of Richard Dyer, whose essay *Entertainment and utopia* provides the basis of her argument, Geraghty insists that the chief function of women's genres is to take five of our most common everyday problems (scarcity, exhaustion, dreariness, manipulation and fragmentation) and then translate them into their much-desired opposites (abundance, energy, intensity, transparency and community). The twist in her argument is that utopian transformations of this sort are usually effected by female characters, whom we admire all the more as a result. Here are some of her examples:

(a) the way that female characters in *Dallas*, such as Alexis and Krystle, create an impression of abundance with their expensive clothes and 'endless consumerism'

(b) the way that many of *Coronation Street*'s best-loved *femmes fatales*, including Elsie Tanner and Bet Lynch, have conveyed an air of emotional honesty or 'transparency' in their more tragic scenes

(c) the way that, in a variety of British soaps (*Coronation Street, East Enders, Brookside*), it is usually strong women who hold families together, and hence reinforce the prevailing sense of community.

Analysing the audience

But what about the attempt to prove that the audience for women's genres is altogether more creative and intelligent than is usually supposed? It is here that British writers have really excelled. The classic work of audience analysis is Dorothy Hobson's *Crossroads: The Drama of a Soap Opera* (1982), based on an ethnographic investigation of a cross section of women who regularly watched the soap opera *Crossroads*. It would be impossible to summarise the whole of Hobson's extremely nuanced account of women's viewing habits, so we will concentrate here on four of her most important themes.

Consuming creatively

Hobson's chief objective is to emphasise the considerable mental dexterity which women exhibit when they respond to soap operas. She points out, in the first place, that many women are unable to watch attentively when their favourite soaps are being broadcast, because they tend to give priority to domestic chores (note that *Crossroads* usually went out at tea time). This means that they are forced to use aural clues, such as the voices of the actors and the various background noises, in order to conjure a mental picture of the unfolding action. Soap operas make this possible because they use the same characters and the same locations for week after week.

Of even greater importance is women's skill in responding to the narrative element of soap operas. Hobson argues that it is rare for women to concentrate solely on the events of a single episode, because they are normally very good at following an unfolding story over a very extended period. She suggests that this might be a sort of residual talent inherited from pre-modern times, when women would try to allay the boredom of domestic labour by telling each other long and highly complicated tales

Adapting to difficult circumstances
One of Hobson's most persistent themes is the ingenious way in which women use media texts to help them cope with difficult domestic circumstances. In her book on *Crossroads*, for instance, she concentrates on the plight of young mothers bringing up children on their own, and suggests that the programme helps them in at least three ways:

- First, by virtue of being broadcast at the same time everyday, it can serve as a fixed point which enables the women to construct a daily routine.

- Second, it serves as an antidote to loneliness by allowing the women to keep up with long-established characters whom they regard as their friends.

- Third, its continuous narratives create a powerful sense of life being lived more purposefully elsewhere, which compensates the women for the feeling that they have become stuck in a domestic rut.

Addressing problems
We have already seen how Christine Geraghty defends soap operas against the charge of escapism, but how does Hobson approach the same issue?
She accepts that there is an escapist element in soap opera, but insists that most women tend to be mildly critical when it becomes excessive. More importantly, however, she also claims that soap

operas are especially effective in persuading women to think seriously about social problems. This is because problems such as rape, alcoholism and poverty are shown affecting characters whom the audience cares about deeply, and therefore seem more 'real' than when presented in abstract form on a non-fiction programme.

So she almost tends to see soap opera as a form of social realism?
Not entirely. Although Hobson is very sympathetic to the way soap operas address social problems, she accepts that their treatment of them will usually be tainted by escapism in the end. Her claim, more precisely, is that they usually provide 'magical' rather than real solutions to the problems which they raise.

Can you give an example of what she means?
At the time when Hobson was researching her book, one of the storylines in *Crossroads* concerned a repressed young woman called Alison who became pregnant after her first sexual experience. This put her in an impossible position, because her religious convictions made it unthinkable for her to have an abortion, even though she recognised that she was in no position to look after a child. And yet, as Hobson points out, her dilemma was magically resolved after a few episodes when she suffered a miscarriage.

Voicing an opinion
Hobson wrote her book on *Crossroads* at a time when Noele Gordon, the actress who played the character of Meg Richardson, was being written out of the series. This event provoked an extraordinary protest from viewers, who inundated the programme's production company with angry letters demanding Gordon's reinstatement. When Hobson examined the protest in detail, she was particularly struck by three things:

- First, since the women felt thoroughly familiar with *Crossroads* (not least because it was broadcast so often), they took it for granted that they were entitled to have their say about the programme's future.

- Second, the protest was violently anti-elitist in both content and tone, with many of the viewers demanding the resignation of the head of the channel which broadcast *Crossroads*.

- Third, the protest was also underpinned by a sort of instinctive cultural relativism, in the sense that many viewers questioned the right of media professionals to impose their artistic choices on other people.

The importance of the protest, in Hobson's opinion, was that it implicitly raised the question of whether it is still tenable to maintain a rigid distinction between the minority who produce culture and the majority who consume it. Whereas some might regard the campaign to 'save' Noele Gordon as evidence only of mindless fanaticism, Hobson sees it as an inspiring precursor of one of the intellectual left's most deeply-cherished ambitions: the establishment of cultural democracy.

Transforming culture

The new social movements have never confined themselves to simply analysing culture. They have also proved remarkably effective at making cultural interventions of their own. If we think of the various ways in which the feminist movement has tried to intervene in contemporary culture, there are three which stand out:

1. It has campaigned against aspects of mainstream culture which it regards as especially oppressive towards women (pornography is the obvious example).

2. It has drawn attention to the work of women artists who have been 'written out' of cultural history.

3. It has produced cultural texts of its own.

There is broad support in Cultural Studies for the idea of a feminist intervention in modern culture, but there have also been major disagreements over the form it should take. Several writers have exposed the activities listed above to critical analysis, claiming that they have sometimes been based on shaky cultural assumptions and that they have often had negative consequences for the feminist movement as a whole. The best way of illustrating this important strand in Cultural Studies is to examine Michele Barrett's essay *Feminism and the Definition of Cultural Politics*, first published in 1982.

Opposing censorship

Barrett's first target is what she regards as the feminist movement's oversimplified approach to the issue of representation. She is especially troubled by the way that certain works tend to be dismissed as self-evidently sexist, whereas others are greeted as self-evidently progressive. Her own belief is that the same text will often have different effects on different people. Much will depend on the circumstances in which it is encountered and on the attitude of the person who encounters it. By way of an example, she recalls an occasion on which a play depicting rape was staged at her own college. Most of the audience consisted of feminists, who treated the rape scene as a powerful exposure of patriarchy; but there were also a number of rugby players present who treated the whole thing as a huge joke.

Two points can be made about this aspect of Barrett's work. The first is that it is clearly indebted to the ideas about polysemy which have been central to Cultural Studies. The second is that it allows her to oppose the demand for censorship which has characterised many feminist campaigns against mainstream culture, especially in the case of pornography. Barrett accepts that pornography poses a threat to women, but argues that any attempt to censor it would conflict with the democratic ethos which feminism tries to embody. By showing that the same text can have different effects in different circumstances, she deprives the pro-censorship lobby of one of its most powerful arguments.

Recovering texts

Barrett turns now to the second of the activities listed above, namely the attempt by feminists to 'recover' the work of women artists who have otherwise been forgotten. She accepts that this has often had positive results (not least by conveying a 'real sense of women's achievements'), but she also argues that it frequently seems to conflict with wider feminist objectives. She points out, for instance, that:

(a) The work of most women artists has rarely expressed a feminist perspective. There is arguably no political advantage in making it available again.

(b) There is a limit to the amount of work which women produced in the past. This means that certain feminists have tried to widen the definition of female creativity, so that activities like knitting and embroidery can be used to supplement works of art. The problem with this approach is that it reinforces the assumption that most women's activity is domestic.

(c) Modern researchers have tended to arrange the work of women artists in strict hierarchies. This is inconsistent with the feminist belief in egalitarianism.

Redefining art

So much for the art of the past. But what about the attempt by modern artists to create work which expresses a feminist perspective? Barrett is more enthusiastic about this aspect of feminist cultural politics, but she is critical of some of the aesthetic assumptions which appear to underpin it. She is especially concerned that women artists are still attached to a romantic conception of art, which holds that creativity is inherently mysterious and that all artists are geniuses. The problem with this approach, she goes on to argue, is that it divides us culturally into the talented few and the 'untalented majority', in a way which is again inconsistent with the feminist belief in equality.

Her solution is to argue for a new conception of art, based on the related ideas of **skill** and **imagination**. Instead of agreeing that creativity is fundamentally mysterious, feminists should affirm that all works of art are actually the product of identifiable skills which other people can learn. They should also seek to revive the idea that the primary function of art is to create fictional realities by using the imagination. If this occurs, Barrett argues, then the cultural politics of feminism will be transformed in two major ways:

> *First* – The emphasis on skill will help to 'demystify' the arts and create a more equal relationship between feminist artists and their audience.
>
> *Second* – The emphasis on imagination will affirm that the main objective of art is to provide *pleasure*, and will therefore remind feminist artists that it is as important to intervene in popular culture as to experiment with avant-garde styles.

Barrett's essay may not represent the last word on feminist cultural politics, but it serves as a powerful model of what academic critics can do when they seek to intervene in contemporary culture. It reminds us that the ultimate purpose of Cultural Studies has always been to analyse culture with a view to changing it. This is the point you should bear in mind as we bring our introductory survey to an end.

Helping you learn

Progress questions

1. Are critics like Morag Schiach right to argue that Cultural Studies has often been guilty of unconscious sexism?

2. In what ways have feminist writers tried to rescue 'women's genres' from the disdain in which they are currently held?

3. How convincing is Michele Barrett's attempt to clarify the conceptual foundations of feminist cultural politics?

Seminar discussion

1. How creative are you when you watch your favourite soap opera?

2. Should feminists campaign for the censorship of pornography?

Practical assignment

Try and identify some of the ways in which the perceived male bias of Cultural Studies could be challenged.

Study and revision tips

1. Try and read some of the literature by women that feminist critics have 'rescued' from historical oblivion.

2. There are many different schools of feminism. Find something out about each of them.

Further Reading

This is a brief reading list which contains a few key books and articles relevant to the various topics we have examined. Be prepared to look for other material in your college library when writing essays or revising for exams.

Chapter 1: Understanding Culture

Will Brooker, *Teach Yourself Cultural Studies* (Hodder and Stoughton, 1998).

Dennis Dworkin, *Cultural Marxism in Postwar Britain: History, the New Left, and the Origins of Cultural Studies* (Duke University Press, 1997).

Angela McRobbie, 'Let's hear it for cultural studies' in the *New Statesman*, 14 February 1997.

Ziauddin Sardar, 'Stop studying cultural studies' in the *New Statesman*, 7 March 1997.

Ziauddin Sardar and Borin Van Loon, *Cultural Studies for Beginners* (Icon Books, 1997).

Graeme Turner, *British Cultural Studies: An Introduction* (Unwin Hyman, 1990).

John Storey (ed), *Cultural Theory and Popular Culture: A Reader* (Harvester Wheatsheaf, 1994).

Chapter 2: The New Left

FR Leavis and Denys Thompson, *Culture and Environment* (Chatto and Windus, 1959, first published 1933).

Alan O' Connor, *Raymond Williams: Writing, Culture, Politics* (Blackwell, 1989).

Raymond Williams, *Culture and Society 1780–1950* (Penguin, 1979, first published 1958).

Raymond Williams, *The Long Revolution* (Penguin, 1984, first published 1961).

Raymond Williams, *Communications* (Penguin, 1966, first published 1962).

Raymond Williams, 'Culture is Ordinary' in *Resources of Hope* (Verso, 1988).

Chapter 3: Media Analysis

James Curran, 'Capitalism and control of the press 1800–1975' in James Curran, Michael Gurevitch and Janet Woollacott (eds), *Mass Communication and Society* (Edward Arnold, 1977).

James Curran and Jean Seaton, *Power Without Responsibility: The Press and Broadcasting in Britain* (Routledge, fifth edition, 1997).

Stuart Hall, 'Encoding/Decoding' in Stuart Hall, Dorothy Hobson, Andrew Lowe and Paul Willis (eds), *Culture, Media, Language* (Hutchinson, 1980).

Graham Murdock and Peter Golding, 'For a Political Economy of Mass Communications' in Ralph Miliband and John Saville (eds), *The Socialist Register 1973* (Merlin Press, 1974).

Graham Murdock and Peter Golding, 'Capitalism, Communication and Class Relations' in James Curran, Michael Gurevitch and Janet Woollacott (eds), *Mass Communication and Society* (Edward Arnold, 1977).

Chapter 4: Subcultures

Iain Chambers, *Urban Rhythms: Pop Music and Popular Culture* (Macmillan, 1985).

Stuart Hall and Tony Jefferson (eds), *Resistance through Rituals: Youth Subcultures in Post-War Britain* (Hutchinson, 1976).

Stewart Home, *The Assault on Culture: Utopian Currents from Lettrisme to Class War* (Aporia Press,1988).

Dick Hebdige, *Subculture: The Meaning of Style* (Methuen, 1979).

George McKay, 'CRASS 621984 ANOK4U2' in *Senseless Acts of Beauty: Cultures of Resistance since the Sixties* (Verso, 1996).

Steve Redhead (ed), *Rave Off: Politics and deviance in contemporary youth culture* (Avebury, 1993).

Jon Savage, *England's Dreaming: Sex Pistols and Punk Rock* (Faber and Faber, 1991).

Chapter 5: *Screen*

Louis Althusser, 'Ideology and Ideological State Apparatuses' in *Lenin and Philosophy and Other Essays* (New Left Books, 1971).

Richard Dyer, *Stars* (BFI, 1979).

Richard Dyer, *Heavenly Bodies: Film Stars and Society* (BFI, 1986).

Colin MacCabe, 'Realism and the Cinema: Notes on Some Brechtian Theses' in Antony Easthope (ed), *Contemporary Film Theory* (Longman, 1993).

Laura Mulvey, 'Visual Pleasure and Narrative Cinema' in Antony

Easthope (ed), *Contemporary Film Theory* (Longman, 1993).
Peter Wollen, 'Godard and counter-cinema: *Vent d'Est*' in *Readings and Writings* (Verso, 1982).

Chapter 6: Thatcherism and 'New Times'

Jean Baudrillard, 'The Ecstasy of Communication' in Hal Foster (ed), *Postmodern Culture* (Pluto Press, 1985).
John Docker, *Postmodernism and Popular Culture: A Cultural History* (Cambridge University Press, 1994).
Stuart Hall, *The Hard Road to Renewal: Thatcherism and the Crisis of the Left* (Verso, 1988).
Stuart Hall, 'A torpedo aimed at the boiler-room of consensus' in the *New Statesman*, 17 April 1988.
Stuart Hall, Charles Critcher, Tony Jefferson, John Clarke and Brian Roberts, *Policing the Crisis: Mugging, the State and Law and Order* (Macmillan, 1978).
Stuart Hall and Martin Jacques (eds), *New Times: The Changing Face of Politics in the 1990s* (Lawrence and Wishart, 1989).
Fredric Jameson, 'Postmodernism and Consumer Society' in E Ann Kaplan (ed), *Postmodernism and Its Discontents: Theories, Practices* (Verso, 1988).
Jean-Francois Lyotard, *The Postmodern Condition: A report on knowledge* (Manchester University Press, 1986).
Kobena Mercer, '1968: Periodizing Politics and Identity' in Lawrence Grossberg, Cary Nelson, Paula Treichler (eds), *Cultural Studies* (Routledge, 1992).

Chapter 7: Cultural Populism

John Fiske, *Understanding Popular Culture* (Unwin Hyman, 1989).
John Fiske, *Reading the Popular* (Unwin Hyman, 1989).
Jim McGuigan, *Cultural Populism* (Routledge, 1992).
Paul Willis, *Common Culture* (Routledge, 1990).
Paul Willis, *Moving Culture: An enquiry into the cultural activities of young people* (Calouste Gulbenkian Foundation, 1990).

Chapter 8: New Social Movements

Ien Ang, *Watching Dallas: Soap opera and the melodramatic imagination* (Methuen, 1985).
Michele Barrett, 'Feminism and the Definition of Cultural Politics' in Rosalind Brunt and Caroline Rowan (eds), *Feminism, Culture and Politics* (Lawrence and Wishart, 1982).

Christine Geraghty, *Women and Soap Opera* (Polity Press, 1991).
Dorothy Hobson, 'Housewives and the Mass Media' in Stuart Hall, Dorothy Hobson, Andrew Lowe and Paul Willis (eds), *Culture, Media, Language* (Hutchinson, 1980).
Dorothy Hobson, *Crossroads: The Drama of a Soap Opera* (Methuen, 1982).
Angela McRobbie, 'Settling Accounts with Subcultures: A Feminist Critique' in Simon Frith and Andrew Goodwin (eds), *On Record: Rock, Pop and the Written Word* (Routledge, 1990).
Morag Schiach, 'Feminism and Popular Culture' in John Storey (ed), *Cultural Theory and Popular Culture: A Reader* (Harvester Wheatsheaf, 1994).

Glossary

aesthetics The study of the nature of art and related topics (e.g. beauty).
anti-aesthetics The belief that it is necessary to destroy the arts and other forms of representation, usually on the grounds that they constitute a barrier to political progress.
authoritarian populism Stuart Hall's term for the politics of Thatcherism.
avant-garde Experimentalism in the arts.
bourgeoisie Term used by Marxists to refer to the 'ruling class' in capitalist society.
bricolage Claude Levi-Strauss's term for the practice of changing an objects's meaning by altering its context.
canon The body of artistic and intellectual works which are generally held to be of special merit or significance.
CCCS Centre for Contemporary Cultural Studies at Birmingham University (now known as the Department of Cultural Studies and Sociology).
common culture A culture shared by a whole society.
conjunctural crisis Antonio Gramsci's term for periods when several different levels of society are simultaneously destabilised.
counter cinema Term used by *Screen* magazine to refer to the work of experimental directors such as Jean-Luc Godard.
critique The criticism of an existing body of ideas.
cultural imperialism The process by which one nation achieves cultural dominance over another.
cultural populism Name applied to a body of work in Cultural Studies which leans towards the uncritical celebration of popular culture.
cultural relativism The idea that there are no 'objective' grounds on which to assert that one cultural text is better than another.
Dadaism One of the earliest and most influential anti-aesthetic movements.
decoding The process by which cultural texts are interpreted.
detournement Term employed by the SI to describe the method of

satirising works of art by rearranging their contents.

diegesis Material which relates to the narrative content of a film.

egalitarian Expressive of a belief in equality.

encoding The process by which cultural texts are produced.

evasion John Fiske's term for the way that audiences respond 'offensively' to popular texts.

genres Texts whose content is determined by a recognisable set of conventions (e.g. Westerns, thrillers).

hegemony Antonio Gramsci's term for the way that the ruling groups achieve dominance by making strategic concessions to the outlook of subordinate groups.

historical materialism The Marxist theory of history.

hyper-reality Jean Baudrillard's term for the profusion of images which surrounds us in postmodern societies.

ideology Either (a) a set of ideas, or (b) a set of ideas whose main purpose is to win support for the existing social order.

interpellation Louis Althusser's term for the way that ideology positions 'individuals as subjects'.

intertextuality The interrelationship between different texts.

Marxism Political philosophy derived from the work of Karl Marx (1818–1883) and Frederick Engels (1820–1895).

metalanguage The voice of the author in a text.

metanarrative Jean-Francois Lyotard's term for the 'universalising' ideologies of the modern period, such as liberalism and Marxism.

MIPC The Manchester Institute of Popular Culture, based at Manchester Metropolitan University.

New Right Neo-conservative movement which has emerged in most Western societies over the last 30 years, exemplified by Thatcherism in Britain.

New Times Term used by some writers in Cultural Studies to denote the emergence of 'post-Fordism' in economics and 'postmodernism' in culture.

Nouvelle Vague (New Wave) One of the most important movements in French cinema during the late 1950s and 1960s, led by such directors as Francois Truffaut and Jean-Luc Godard.

object language The voices of the characters in a text.

oceanic consciousness Term used by the psychologist CG Jung to denote states of consciousness in which the distinction between the self and external reality becomes blurred.

paternalism The belief that it is legitimate for an elite to impose its judgements on everyone else.

polysemy The idea that texts contain more than one meaning.
popular culture The culture of the majority of people in any given society, usually defined against 'high' or 'elite' culture.
post-Fordism The prevailing mode of capitalist organisation in most Western societies, at least according to the theory of New Times.
postmodernism The cultural component of New Times.
productivity John Fiske's term for the way that audiences consciously rearrange popular texts to express progressive meanings.
progressive John Fiske's term for decodings which emphasise small-scale challenges to the dominant ideology, as opposed to large-scale efforts to transform the entire social system.
punk The most important youth subculture of the 1970s.
realism The belief that cultural texts can convey a more or less accurate impression of reality.
scopophilia Freud's term for pleasure in looking, used by Laura Mulvey in her work on the representation of women in film.
SI Situationist International.
socialism Political movement which (a) supports the institutions of the labour movement such as the trade unions, and (b) aims either to abolish or reform the capitalist system.
Spectacle The SI's term for the network of images which surrounds us in 'media society'.
structuralism The intellectual movement derived from the work of the structural linguist Ferdinand de Saussure (1875–1913).
subculture Youth groups such as the mods, skinheads and punks which tend to exist in opposition to mainstream culture.
symbolic creativity Paul Willis's term for the inventive way in which ordinary people allegedly use popular texts.
symbolic resistance The term used by the CCCS to denote the various ways in which subcultures express their opposition to the established society.
Thatcherism The body of ideas associated with the British politician Margaret Thatcher, Conservative Prime Minister between 1979 and 1990.
utopian Pertaining to an ideal or better world.

Web sites for students

The following list of web sites will help you increase your knowledge of the topics examined in this book. It is divided into two sections:

- general sites
- sites on specific topics

General sites

Bad Subjects
http://english-server.hss.cmu.edu/bs/
This is a highly political site which often publishes articles by many of the leading figures in American Cultural Studies, such as Cornel West.

Birmingham Department of Cultural Studies and Sociology
http://www.bham.ac.uk/culturalstudies
A site compiled by the successor department to the CCCS.

Cultural Studies and Critical Theory
http://english-www.hss.cmu.edu/theory/
This focuses on the role of critical theory in a wide range of academic disciplines, Cultural Studies included.

Cultural Studies and Media Culture
http://www.gseis.ucla.edu/courses/ed253a/253webb.htm
This site, compiled at the University of California at Los Angeles, contains the online journal *Cultural Studies West*.

Cultural Studies Central
http://home.earthlink.net/~markowitz/
Provides an outlet for the idiosyncratic opinions of the critic Robin Markowitz.

Culture and Communication Reading Room
http://kali.murdoch.edu.au/~cntinuum/index1.htm/
The site is compiled by the Centre for Research in Culture and Communication at Murdoch University, Australia. It is especially good on cultural policy.

Media and Communications Site
http://www.aber.ac.uk/~dgc/media.htm
This contains the web site of the Association for Media, Communication and Cultural Studies.

The Media and Communication Studies Site
http://www.aber.ac.uk/~dgc/ukdepts.html
Contains a useful list of most of the courses in Cultural, Media and Communication Studies currently offered by British institutions of Higher Education.

Manchester Institute for Popular Culture
http://darion.mmu.ac.uk./h&ss/mipc/home.htm
Site compiled by the academic department which has made the central contribution to the analysis of rave culture.

Voice of the Shuttle
http://humanitas.ucsb.edu/shuttle/cultural.htm/
This is by far the most useful internet resource in the field of Cultural Studies. It contains links to hundreds of relevant sites.

Sites on specific topics

A White Brit Rave Aesthete Thinks Aloud
http://members.aol.com/blissout/front.htm
A site devoted to writings on rave culture by the British critic Simon Reynolds, author of *Energy Flash.*

Conditions of Their Own Making
http://hoshi.cic.sfu.ca/calj/cjc/backissues/18.schulman.htm/
Contains a useful article by Norma Schulman on the history of the CCCS, originally published in the *Canadian Journal of Communications.*

Stuart Hall Page
http://www.tiac.net/users/thaslett/s_hall/hall_index.htm/

Interesting information on the former Director of the CCCS.

Institute for Advanced Technology in the Humanities
http://jefferson.village.virginia.edu/pmc
This is a general site, compiled at the University of Virginia in Charlottesville, but it is chiefly of interest for its online journal *Postmodern Culture*.

Issues in European Politics: Post-Fordism
http://www.king.ac.uk/~se-s411/issues/bib981.htm
Contains a useful reading list of books and articles on post-Fordism.

John Fiske
http://www.wisc.edu/commarts/depart/faculty/fiske.htm
Homepage compiled by the high priest of cultural populism.

Louis Althusser: Ideology and Ideological State Apparatuses
http://www.spc.uchicago.edu/ssrl/prelims/strat/stadd.htm/#althusser
Provides the complete text of Althusser's most influential essay on ideology.

Marx and Engels WWW Library
http://csf.Colorado.edu/psn/marx/archive/
Extraordinary research tool which aims to make the complete works of Marx and Engels available online.

Marxist Media Theory
http://www.aber.ac.uk/~dgc/marxism.html
Useful guide by Daniel Chandler to the whole range of Marxist approaches to the media.

The New Left and Cultural Theory
http://www.warwick.ac.uk./fac/arts/english/wip/kav311.htm/
An interesting interview with Fred Inglis, Raymond Williams's biographer, on the contribution of the New Left to the early history of Cultural Studies.

Paul Willis
http://www.sub.su.se/sam/nyri/young/y933rev1.htm
Contains a thought-provoking review of Willis's book *Common Culture*.

Resources on Antonio Gramsci
http://www.soc.qc.edu/gramsci/

Site devoted to the Italian thinker whose influence on British Cultural Studies has been fundamental.

Semiotics for Beginners
http://www.aber.ac.uk/~dgc/sem01.html
Valuable introduction to the so-called 'science of signs' by Daniel Chandler.

Situationist International
http://ernie.bgsu.edu/~swilbur/si.htm/
This is a site devoted to the organisation of 'cultural saboteurs' whose ideas had a powerful influence on the punk movement.

Studymates

Studymates
http://www.studymates.co.uk
Look for Cultural Studies on the Studymates web site, to access the links given in this appendix.

Index